ONE MIX
A HUNDRED
DISHES

ONE MIX
A HUNDRED
DISHES

Linda Doeser

Written by Linda Doeser
Photography by Clive Bozzard-Hill
Cover design by Geoff Borin
Home economy by Valerie Barrett

Notes for the Reader
This book uses both metric and imperial measurements. Follow the same units of measurement
throughout; do not mix metric and imperial. All spoon measurements are level: teaspoons are
assumed to be 5 ml, and tablespoons are assumed to be 15 ml. Unless otherwise stated, milk is
assumed to be full fat, eggs and individual vegetables are medium, and pepper is freshly ground
black pepper. Unless otherwise stated, all root vegetables should be washed in plain water and
peeled prior to using.

For best results, use a food thermometer when cooking meat and poultry – check the latest
government guidelines for current advice. Garnishes, decorations and serving suggestions are
all optional and not necessarily included in the recipe ingredients or method. The times given are
an approximate guide only. Preparation times differ according to the techniques used by different
people and the cooking times may also vary from those given. Optional ingredients, variations or
serving suggestions have not been included in the time calculations.

Recipes using raw or very lightly cooked eggs should be avoided by infants, the elderly, pregnant
women, convalescents and anyone suffering from an illness. Pregnant and breastfeeding women are
advised to avoid eating peanuts and peanut products. Sufferers from nut allergies should be aware
that some of the ready-made ingredients used in the recipes in this book may contain nuts. Always
check the packaging before use.

Contents

Introduction

One of the best things about minced beef is its versatility. It goes with a vast range of ingredients to create a wide variety of different meals from burgers to pasta sauces and from stuffed vegetables to pastry turnovers. Its most immediately obvious partners are onions and garlic and, perhaps, tomatoes, mushrooms and herbs, but it responds to a multitude of flavours and textures, whether hot or aromatic spices, peas and beans, many kinds of cheese, a huge array of vegetables and lots of ready-made sauces and condiments, from soy sauce to mustard. Perhaps surprisingly, it even combines well with fruit, such as apples and raisins.

As a general rule, the basic mince mix (see page 10) works in one of two ways. The raw ingredients can be mixed together until thoroughly combined and then shaped into meatballs, burgers, dumplings, kebabs, croquettes, pie fillings or meatloaf before cooking. Alternatively, the various ingredients can be cooked in a saucepan or casserole so that the flavours mingle deliciously for pasta sauces, braises, stews, curries, gratins and even soups. However, there are still many more variations – all kinds of wraps from omelettes to tortillas, puffs, fritters and muffins, baked and layered dishes and unusual meat and vegetable rolls.

Quality & Economy

Minced beef is undoubtedly an economical choice for family meals, not least because a little can go a long way. This is especially true when it is combined with other ingredients, such as breadcrumbs, to make meatballs or burgers, or when it is served with plenty of filling carbohydrate, such as pasta or a mashed potato topping. It is easy to cook – in the following pages there are 100 easy-to-follow tasty recipes for all occasions – and it is popular with adults and children alike.

However, the quality of minced beef can vary widely and buying the cheapest you can find may often prove to be a false economy. Many supermarkets sell 'bargain' packs and although the meat may look perfectly satisfactory, it usually contains quite a high percentage of fat. Not only is this less healthy, it is also wasteful. In the long run, meat labelled 'premium' or minced steak is a better and more economical choice. Minced steak from a good local butcher is probably the best choice of all.

Supermarkets will often have special offers on beef mince, and you can certainly make savings on this versatile ingredient. However, it doesn't keep for long in the refrigerator, but raw meat can be frozen for up to three months. Many cooked dishes, such as Bolognese sauce, also freeze well, so batch cooking is a good way to save both money and time.

When buying fresh beef mince, check the use-by date and make sure that the pack isn't damaged and is properly sealed. Store on a low shelf in the refrigerator, away from cooked foods and ingredients intended to be eaten raw. If the pack is damaged or you have bought it loose from the butcher, remove the packaging and transfer the meat to a covered dish and store in the refrigerator. Ideally, fresh beef mince should be cooked and eaten on the day of purchase.

Minced beef will always contain some fat. This is why it is easy to brown in a non-stick pan without adding any oil – a technique that is the perfect start for many recipes. For some recipes, it is very important to drain off as much fat as possible after browning the meat – with or without additional oil – as the mixture needs to be quite dry. In fact, it is always worth checking the pan after browning minced beef and, if it does look a bit greasy, draining off the excess.

Equipment

All the recipes in this book can be prepared and cooked with the tools and equipment found in most kitchens – scales, chopping boards, knives, saucepans and frying pans, mixing bowls and so on. The only specialist pan suggested in one or two recipes is a wok – a large pan with sloping sides designed for stir-frying – but you can use a frying pan instead, although it is not quite so easy to keep the ingredients moving while they cook.

It is worth buying the best-quality pans you can afford because, if you look after them well, they will last many years. A pan with a thick, solid base, preferably ground rather than stamped flat, distributes heat well so that the food cooks evenly. Make sure that the handles are secure and lids fit tightly. Always use the correct-sized pan as one that is too small may cause ingredients to cook unevenly or boil over, while

one that is too large may result in the dish drying out. A flameproof casserole is extremely useful and can double as a large saucepan.

It is also worth buying good-quality knives and an efficient sharpener. Keep knives sharp, as not only are they more efficient when sharp, but they are also much safer. Blunt knives can easily slip and cut your hand. Store them in a knife block or a wall-mounted magnetic rack out of the reach of children. Do not store them in a drawer where other tools may damage the cutting edges. Always use a wooden or polyethylene chopping board when slicing or dicing, as hard materials, such as glass, metal or granite, can damage the blades.

About the Basic Mince Mix

As beef mince is so versatile, the basic mince mix is very flexible and easily adapted. Onions always feature, but in some recipes a different member of the onion family, such as shallots or spring onions, is substituted. Garlic is a valuable addition in many dishes, but it is optional as some people find its flavour too pungent.

Herbs, spices and flavourings are added to the basic mix to give each dish its unique character and quantities vary from a pinch to several tablespoons, depending on the strength of flavour. A huge range features throughout the book – fresh and dried herbs, hot and aromatic spices, sauces and condiments, fresh and dried chillies, to name just a few. Other additional ingredients, such as stock, canned or fresh tomatoes, potatoes, breadcrumbs and mushrooms, vary according to the type of dish.

Basic Mince Mix

Serves 4–6

* 1 kg/2 lb 4 oz fresh beef mince
* 1 onion, finely chopped (recipes may substitute
    Spanish onions, red onions, shallots or
    spring onions)
* 1 garlic clove, finely chopped (optional)
* salt and pepper

This is the basic mix that all 100 variations of minced beef dishes in the book are based on.

For each recipe the basic mix is highlighted (✻) for easy reference, so then all you have to do is follow the easy steps each time and a world of delicious and tempting meals will await you.

Please note that the ingredient quantities vary from time to time so please check these carefully.

Easy

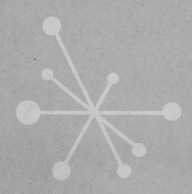

Beef & Tomato Soup

1. Heat the oil in a large saucepan. Add the onion and garlic and cook over a low heat, stirring occasionally, for 5 minutes, until softened. Stir in the chillies and tomatoes and cook for a further 5 minutes. Add the beef, increase the heat to medium and cook, breaking it up with a wooden spoon, for 6–8 minutes, until lightly browned.

2. Stir in the carrots, potatoes and parsley, pour in the stock and season to taste with salt and pepper. Bring to the boil, then reduce the heat, cover and simmer for 30 minutes, until the meat and vegetables are tender.

3. Taste and adjust the seasoning, adding salt and pepper if needed. Ladle the soup into warmed bowls, garnish with parsley and serve immediately with crusty rolls.

Serves 6

3 tbsp sunflower oil

* 1 onion, finely chopped

* 1 garlic clove, finely chopped

2 fresh red chillies, deseeded and finely chopped

4 large tomatoes, peeled and chopped

* 500 g/1 lb 2 oz fresh beef mince

2 carrots, diced

2 potatoes, diced

1–2 tbsp chopped fresh flat-leaf parsley, plus extra to garnish

1.2 litres/2 pints beef stock

* salt and pepper

crusty rolls, to serve

Home-made Burgers

1. Put the beef, onion, parsley and Worcestershire sauce into a bowl, season to taste with salt and pepper and mix well with your hands until thoroughly combined.

2. Divide the mixture into six equal portions and shape into balls, then gently flatten into patties. If you have time, chill in the refrigerator for 30 minutes to firm up.

3. Heat the oil in a large frying pan. Add the burgers, in batches, and cook over a medium heat for 5–8 minutes on each side, turning them carefully with a fish slice. Remove from the pan and keep warm while you cook the remaining burgers.

4. Serve in toasted buns with lettuce leaves, tomato slices, gherkins and tomato ketchup.

Serves 6

✳ 1 kg/2 lb 4 oz fresh beef mince
✳ 1 small onion, grated
1 tbsp chopped fresh parsley
2 tsp Worcestershire sauce
2 tbsp sunflower oil
✳ salt and pepper

To serve
6 burger buns, split and toasted
lettuce leaves
tomato slices
gherkins, sliced
tomato ketchup

Beef & Bacon Burgers

1. Preheat the grill. Put the beef, onion, garlic (if using), breadcrumbs, sage and egg into a bowl, season to taste with salt and pepper and mix well until thoroughly combined. Divide the mixture into six equal portions and shape into balls, then gently flatten into patties.

2. Wrap a bacon rasher around each patty and secure with a wooden cocktail stick.

3. Brush one side of each burger with a little of the melted butter and cook under the preheated grill for 5 minutes. Carefully turn the burgers with a spatula, brush with the remaining melted butter and grill for a further 4–5 minutes, until cooked to your liking.

4. Carefully transfer the burgers to warmed individual plates, then remove and discard the cocktail sticks. Serve immediately.

Serves 6

* 650 g/1 lb 7 oz fresh beef mince
* 1 large onion, very finely chopped
* 1 garlic clove, very finely chopped (optional)

  85 g/3 oz fresh breadcrumbs

  2 tsp chopped fresh sage

  1 large egg, lightly beaten

  6 bacon rashers

  40 g/1½ oz butter, melted

* salt and pepper

Beef Keftas

1. Put the beef, onion, garlic, coriander and spices into a bowl and season to taste with salt and pepper. Add the egg and mix well with your hands until thoroughly combined and very smooth. Cover the bowl with clingfilm and chill in the refrigerator for 30 minutes.

2. Meanwhile, mix together the chopped mint and the yogurt in a bowl and season to taste with salt. Cover with clingfilm and chill until required.

3. Preheat the grill or barbecue. Remove the beef mixture from the refrigerator, scoop up pieces with your hands and shape into small ovals about 2 cm/¾ inch thick. Thread the keftas onto metal or pre-soaked wooden skewers, with three to each skewer.

4. Brush the grill rack or barbecue grill with oil. Cook the skewers, in batches if necessary, under the preheated grill or over hot coals, turning occasionally, for 10–12 minutes, until cooked through. Garnish with mint leaves and lime wedges and serve immediately with the minted yogurt.

Serves 6–8

* 1 kg/2 lb 4 oz fresh beef mince
* 1 Spanish onion, grated
* 3 garlic cloves, very finely chopped

4 tbsp chopped fresh coriander

1 tsp ground cumin

½ tsp ground cinnamon

½ tsp ground turmeric

1 tsp paprika

1 large egg, lightly beaten

3 tbsp finely chopped fresh mint, plus extra leaves to garnish

150 ml/5 fl oz natural yogurt

sunflower oil, for brushing

* salt and pepper

lime wedges, to garnish

Beef with Scrambled Eggs

1. Melt the butter in a large saucepan. Add the onion and garlic and cook over a low heat, stirring occasionally, for 5 minutes, until softened. Add the beef, increase the heat to medium and cook, stirring frequently and breaking it up with a wooden spoon, for 8–10 minutes, until evenly browned.

2. Add the tomatoes and peppers, reduce the heat and simmer, stirring occasionally, for 15 minutes, until the meat and vegetables are tender. Stir in the Worcestershire sauce and parsley and season to taste with salt and pepper.

3. Lightly beat the eggs in a bowl and season to taste with salt and pepper. Add the eggs to the pan and cook, stirring, for a few minutes, until lightly scrambled.

4. Garnish with parsley and serve immediately with toast triangles.

Serves 6

85 g/3 oz butter

* 1 onion, sliced

* 1 garlic clove, finely chopped

* 500 g/1 lb 2 oz fresh beef mince

2 tomatoes, peeled and sliced

1 small red pepper, deseeded and diced

1 small yellow pepper, deseeded and diced

1 tbsp Worcestershire sauce

1 tbsp chopped fresh parsley, plus extra to garnish

6 eggs

* salt and pepper

buttered toast triangles, to serve

Stir-fried Beef

1. Mix together half the rice wine, the garlic, ginger, soy sauce, sesame oil and cornflour in a bowl. Add the beef, turning and stirring to coat, cover with clingfilm and leave to marinate in the refrigerator for 1 hour.

2. Heat a wok over a medium heat, then add the groundnut oil, swirl it around the wok and heat. Remove the beef from the bowl, add it to the wok and stir-fry, breaking it up with a wooden spoon, for 3–5 minutes, until evenly browned.

3. Stir in the remaining rice wine, the hoisin sauce, oyster sauce and vinegar and cook, stirring constantly, for 1 minute.

4. Stir in the carrots, spring onions, broccoli, red pepper and baby corn and stir-fry for a further 3–4 minutes, until the vegetables are tender-crisp. Serve immediately.

Serves 6

6 tbsp Chinese rice wine or dry sherry

3 garlic cloves, very finely chopped

2 tbsp finely chopped fresh ginger

1 tbsp dark soy sauce

1 tsp sesame oil

1 tbsp cornflour

900 g/2 lb fresh beef mince

3 tbsp groundnut oil

2 tbsp hoisin sauce

2 tbsp oyster sauce

2 tsp rice vinegar

2 carrots, thinly sliced diagonally

4 spring onions, thinly sliced lengthways

225 g/8 oz broccoli florets

1 large red pepper, deseeded and thinly sliced

175 g/6 oz baby corn, halved lengthways

Beef & Noodles

1. Cook the noodles according to the packet instructions, then drain and refresh under cold running water. Tip them into a bowl, add 1 tablespoon of the sesame oil and toss to coat.

2. Heat a wok over a medium heat, then add the groundnut oil, swirl it around the wok and heat. Add the onion and stir-fry for a few minutes, until softened. Add the beef and stir-fry, breaking it up with a wooden spoon, for 3–5 minutes, until evenly browned.

3. Stir in the ginger, chilli and five-spice powder and cook, stirring constantly, for 1 minute, then add the carrots, red pepper and mangetout. Stir-fry for a further 4 minutes.

4. Add the beansprouts, the remaining sesame oil and the noodles and stir-fry for a further 2 minutes. Serve immediately.

Serves 6

450 g/1 lb dried egg noodles

2 tbsp sesame oil

2 tbsp groundnut oil

✳ 1 onion, finely chopped

✳ 650 g/1 lb 7 oz fresh beef mince

2.5-cm/1-inch piece fresh ginger, thinly sliced

1 fresh red chilli, deseeded and thinly sliced

1½ tsp Chinese five-spice powder

2 carrots, thinly sliced diagonally

1 red pepper, deseeded and diced

85 g/3 oz mangetout

175 g/6 oz fresh beansprouts

Beef Fried Rice

1. Cook the rice in a large saucepan of salted boiling water for 15 minutes, until tender. Drain the rice, rinse with boiling water and set aside.

2. Heat a wok over a medium heat, then add the groundnut oil, swirl it around the wok and heat. Add the eggs and cook, stirring constantly, for 50–60 seconds, until set. Transfer to a dish and set aside.

3. Add the beef to the wok and stir-fry, breaking it up with a wooden spoon, for 4–5 minutes, until evenly browned. Stir in the onion, garlic and peas and stir-fry for a further 3–4 minutes.

4. Add the rice, soy sauce, sugar and eggs and cook, stirring constantly, for a further 1–2 minutes, until heated through. Serve immediately with prawn crackers.

Serves 6

500 g/1 lb 2 oz long-grain rice

2 tbsp groundnut oil

4 large eggs, lightly beaten

650 g/1 lb 7 oz fresh beef mince

1 large onion, finely chopped

2 garlic cloves, finely chopped

140 g/5 oz frozen peas

3 tbsp light soy sauce

1 tsp sugar

salt

prawn crackers, to serve

Quick Curry

1. Heat half the oil in a large saucepan. Add the onion, green pepper, cumin seeds, cardamom pods and bay leaves and cook over a low heat, stirring constantly, for 2–3 minutes, until the spices give off their aroma. Add the tomatoes and cook, stirring frequently, for 10 minutes.

2. Meanwhile, heat the remaining oil in a frying pan. Add the garlic and cook, stirring frequently, for 1 minute, then add the beef, ground coriander, turmeric and chilli powder. Cook over a medium heat, stirring constantly and breaking up the meat with a wooden spoon, for 4–5 minutes, until the meat is evenly browned. Transfer the mixture to the saucepan.

3. Pour in the stock and bring to the boil, then reduce the heat, cover and simmer, stirring occasionally, for 20–25 minutes. If the mixture seems to be drying out, add a little water.

4. Remove and discard the bay leaves and cardamom pods, then season to taste with salt. Scatter over the chopped coriander and serve immediately with rice and naan bread.

Serves 4

4 tbsp groundnut oil

1 large onion, finely chopped

1 green pepper, deseeded and diced

1 tsp cumin seeds

4 green cardamom pods

2 bay leaves

500 g/1 lb 2 oz tomatoes, peeled and chopped

2 garlic cloves, finely chopped

450 g/1 lb fresh beef mince

2 tsp ground coriander

2 tsp ground turmeric

1 tsp chilli powder

600 ml/1 pint beef stock

2 tbsp chopped fresh coriander

salt

cooked rice and naan bread, to serve

Thai Beef Omelette

1. Heat half the oil in a frying pan. Add the spring onions and garlic and cook over a low heat, stirring occasionally, for 4–5 minutes, until softened. Add the beef, increase the heat to medium and cook, stirring frequently and breaking it up with a wooden spoon, for 5–8 minutes, until evenly browned.

2. Stir in the tomatoes, chilli, sugar and 2 tablespoons of the fish sauce and season to taste with pepper. Reduce the heat and simmer, stirring occasionally, for 15–20 minutes, until thickened and cooked through. Stir in the chopped coriander.

3. Beat the eggs with the remaining fish sauce in a bowl. Heat half the remaining oil in an omelette pan. Add half the egg mixture, tilt the pan to spread it evenly and cook over a low heat for a few minutes, until just set.

4. Spoon half the beef mixture into the centre of the omelette. Using a spatula, fold in the sides to make a neat parcel and slide it out of the pan onto a warmed serving dish. Make a second omelette in the same way with the remaining oil, egg mixture and beef filling. Garnish with coriander sprigs and serve immediately.

Serves 2

4 tbsp groundnut oil

4 spring onions, finely chopped

2 garlic cloves, finely chopped

225 g/8 oz fresh beef mince

2 tomatoes, peeled and chopped

1 fresh red chilli, deseeded and finely chopped

1 tsp sugar

3 tbsp Thai fish sauce

1 tbsp chopped fresh coriander, plus extra sprigs to garnish

6 eggs

pepper

Tex-Mex Pizza

1. Preheat the oven to 200°C/400°F/Gas Mark 6. Brush a baking sheet with oil. Heat the oil in a saucepan. Add the onion and garlic and cook over a low heat, stirring occasionally, for 5 minutes, until softened. Add the beef, increase the heat to medium and cook, stirring frequently and breaking it up with a wooden spoon, for 5–8 minutes, until evenly browned.

2. Drain off any excess fat. Stir in the cumin, jalapeño chillies and refried beans, pour in the water and season to taste with salt. Reduce the heat and simmer gently for 5 minutes, then remove from the heat.

3. Meanwhile, make the pizza dough. Sift the flour and salt into a bowl. Add the butter and rub it in with your fingertips until the mixture resembles breadcrumbs. Pour in 100 ml/3½ fl oz of the milk and mix with a round-bladed knife to a soft dough, adding the remaining milk if necessary. Turn out the dough onto a lightly floured surface and knead gently. Roll out to a 25-cm/10-inch round and transfer to the prepared baking sheet. Push up the edge slightly all around to make a rim.

4. Spread the beef mixture evenly over the pizza base and sprinkle with the cheese. Bake in the preheated oven for 18–20 minutes, until the cheese has melted and is golden. Top with avocado slices, red chilli slices and soured cream and serve immediately.

Serves 2

2 tbsp sunflower oil, plus extra for brushing

* 1 small onion, finely chopped
* 1 garlic clove, finely chopped
* 225 g/8 oz fresh beef mince

1 tsp ground cumin

4 pickled jalapeño chillies, drained and finely chopped

400 g/14 oz canned refried beans

150 ml/5 fl oz water

250 g/9 oz Cheddar cheese, grated

* salt

Pizza dough

175 g/6 oz self-raising flour, plus extra for dusting

pinch of salt

25 g/1 oz butter, cut into small pieces

100–125 ml/3½–4 fl oz milk

To serve

avocado slices

fresh red chilli slices

soured cream

Crispy Beef Fritters

1. Beat the egg yolks in a large bowl until pale and thick. Fold in the beef, onion, baking powder, parsley and Worcestershire sauce and season to taste with salt and pepper. Stir gently until thoroughly combined.

2. Whisk the egg whites in a separate grease-free bowl until stiff, then gently fold them into the beef mixture.

3. Heat the oil in a large frying pan. Drop tablespoonfuls of the beef mixture, about four at a time, into the hot oil and fry for 3 minutes, or until puffed up and brown at the edges. Using a spatula or slotted spoon, turn the fritters over and fry for a further 2–3 minutes.

4. Remove with a slotted spoon and drain on kitchen paper. Keep warm while you cook the remaining fritters, then serve immediately.

Serves 4

4 eggs, separated

* 225 g/8 oz fresh beef mince
* 1 small onion, very finely chopped

½ tsp baking powder

2 tbsp chopped fresh parsley

1 tbsp Worcestershire sauce

4 tbsp sunflower oil

* salt and pepper

One-pot Pasta

1. Heat the oil in a large saucepan with a tight-fitting lid. Add the onion, garlic, celery and carrot and cook over a low heat, stirring occasionally, for 5 minutes, until softened. Add the beef, increase the heat to medium and cook, stirring frequently and breaking it up with a wooden spoon, for 5–8 minutes, until evenly browned.

2. Add the mushrooms and cook for a further 3–4 minutes. Add the tomatoes, tomato purée, sugar, herbs, pasta and wine. Stir in the concentrated stock, add just enough water to cover and stir well.

3. Reduce the heat, cover tightly and simmer gently for 15–20 minutes, until the pasta is tender but still firm to the bite and the sauce has thickened. Season to taste with salt and pepper and serve immediately.

Serves 4

2 tbsp olive oil

1 onion, chopped

1 garlic clove, finely chopped

1 celery stick, chopped

1 carrot, chopped

500 g/1 lb 2 oz fresh beef mince

115 g/4 oz mushrooms, sliced

400 g/14 oz canned chopped tomatoes

1 tbsp tomato purée

1 tsp sugar

pinch of dried oregano

1 tbsp chopped fresh flat-leaf parsley

175 g/6 oz dried fusilli

175 ml/6 fl oz red wine

1½ tbsp concentrated beef stock or 1 beef stock cube

salt and pepper

Cheat's Lasagne

1. Heat the oil in a saucepan. Add the beef, onion, garlic and carrot and cook over a medium heat, stirring frequently and breaking up the meat with a wooden spoon, for 5–8 minutes, until the beef is evenly browned.

2. Stir in the herbs, season to taste with salt and pepper and pour in the passata. Bring to the boil, then reduce the heat, cover and simmer for 15 minutes.

3. Meanwhile, preheat the oven to 190°C/375°F/Gas Mark 5. Mix the ricotta with the egg, stirring until smooth and thoroughly combined.

4. Make alternating layers of the beef mixture, lasagne sheets, ricotta mixture and mozzarella in an ovenproof dish, ending with a layer of mozzarella. Bake in the preheated oven for 40–45 minutes, until the topping is golden and bubbling. Leave to stand for 5 minutes before serving.

Serves 6

2 tbsp olive oil

* 500 g/1 lb 2 oz fresh beef mince

* 1 onion, chopped

* 1 garlic clove, finely chopped

1 carrot, diced

1 tbsp chopped fresh flat-leaf parsley

6 fresh basil leaves, torn

600 ml/1 pint passata

550 g/1 lb 4 oz ricotta cheese

1 egg, lightly beaten

8 no pre-cook lasagne sheets

225 g/8 oz mozzarella cheese, grated

* salt and pepper

Beefy Baked Potatoes

1. Preheat the oven to 220°C/425°F/Gas Mark 7. Prick the potatoes all over with a fork. Put them directly on an oven shelf and bake in the preheated oven for 1¼–1½ hours, until soft.

2. Meanwhile, heat the oil in a saucepan. Add the chopped spring onions and the garlic and cook over a low heat, stirring occasionally for 5 minutes, until softened. Add the beef, increase the heat to medium and cook, stirring frequently and breaking it up with a wooden spoon, for 8–10 minutes, until evenly browned.

3. Stir in the tomato purée, soy sauce and 150 ml/5 fl oz of the stock and season to taste with salt and pepper. Reduce the heat, cover and simmer, stirring occasionally, for 25–30 minutes, adding more stock if the mixture seems to be drying out.

4. Remove the potatoes from the oven and put them on four individual plates. Cut a cross in the centre of each and squeeze gently, then ladle the beef mixture over them. Garnish with shredded spring onions and serve immediately.

Serves 4

4 large baking potatoes
2 tbsp sunflower oil
2 spring onions, finely chopped, plus extra shredded spring onions to garnish
1 garlic clove, finely chopped
350 g/12 oz fresh beef mince
1 tbsp tomato purée
1 tbsp light soy sauce
150–200 ml/5–7 fl oz beef stock
salt and pepper

Battered Beef

1. First, make the batter. Sift the flour, cayenne pepper and salt into a bowl. Make a well in the centre and add the egg and half the milk. Stir together with a wooden spoon, gradually incorporating the dry ingredients, then beat well with a whisk or electric mixer until the batter is smooth and full of bubbles. Stir in the remaining milk, cover with clingfilm and leave to rest for 30 minutes.

2. Meanwhile, preheat the oven to 200°C/400°F/Gas Mark 6. Mix together the beef, onion, garlic and parsley in a bowl and season to taste with salt and pepper.

3. Heat the oil in a shallow baking tin until very hot, then remove from the heat. Stir the batter and pour half of it into the tin. Spread the beef mixture on top, using a spatula, and pour the remaining batter over it.

4. Bake in the preheated oven for 20 minutes, until the batter is bubbling, then reduce the oven temperature to 180°C/350°F/Gas Mark 4. Bake for a further 30 minutes, until golden brown.

5. Garnish with parsley and cut into squares. Serve immediately.

Serves 6

* 650 g/1 lb 7 oz fresh beef mince
* ½ onion, finely chopped
* 1 garlic clove, finely chopped
  1 tbsp finely chopped fresh parsley, plus extra to garnish
  2 tbsp sunflower oil
* salt and pepper

Batter
115 g/4 oz plain flour
pinch of cayenne pepper
pinch of salt
1 large egg
300 ml/10 fl oz milk

Savoury Croquettes

1. Heat the oil in a frying pan. Add the onion and garlic and cook over a low–medium heat, stirring occasionally, for 8–10 minutes, until golden brown.

2. Transfer the onion and garlic to a large bowl, add the beef, one of the eggs, the soured cream, chopped parsley, paprika and 25 g/1 oz of the breadcrumbs and season to taste with salt and pepper. Using your hands, mix well until all the ingredients are thoroughly combined. Shape the mixture into 12 equal-sized croquettes.

3. Lightly beat the remaining eggs in a shallow dish and spread out the remaining breadcrumbs in a separate shallow dish. Coat the croquettes first in beaten egg and then in breadcrumbs.

4. Melt the butter in a large frying pan. Add the croquettes, in batches if necessary, and cook over a medium heat for 5–6 minutes on each side, until evenly browned and cooked through. Remove from the pan with a fish slice and keep warm while you cook the remaining croquettes. Garnish with parsley sprigs and serve immediately.

Serves 6

2 tbsp sunflower oil

* 1 Spanish onion, finely chopped

* 2 garlic cloves, finely chopped

* 1 kg/2 lb 4 oz fresh beef mince

3 eggs

2 tbsp soured cream

1 tbsp chopped fresh flat-leaf parsley, plus extra sprigs to garnish

1 tsp sweet paprika

115 g/4 oz fresh breadcrumbs

85 g/3 oz butter

* salt and pepper

Rissoles

1. Cook the potatoes in a large saucepan of salted boiling water for 25–30 minutes, until tender but not falling apart. Drain well, tip into a bowl and mash until smooth.

2. Add the onion, beef, chives, parsley and Worcestershire sauce and season to taste with salt and pepper. Mix well until thoroughly combined. If you have time, cover the bowl with clingfilm and chill the mixture in the refrigerator for 30–45 minutes to firm up.

3. Dampen your hands and shape the mixture into 12 sausage-shaped rissoles. Lightly beat the eggs in a shallow dish, spread out the flour in a second shallow dish and spread out the breadcrumbs in a third shallow dish.

4. Pour oil into a large frying pan to a depth of about 1 cm/ ½ inch and heat. Meanwhile, coat the rissoles first in the flour, then in the beaten egg and, finally, in the breadcrumbs. Shake off any excess.

5. Add the rissoles to the frying pan, in batches if necessary, and cook over a medium heat, turning occasionally, for 8–10 minutes, until crisp, evenly browned and cooked through. Remove from the pan with a fish slice and keep warm while you cook the remaining rissoles. Serve immediately.

Serves 6

1 kg/2 lb 4 oz potatoes

✳ 1 onion, finely chopped

✳ 500 g/1 lb 2 oz fresh beef mince

1 tbsp snipped fresh chives

1 tbsp chopped fresh parsley

2 tsp Worcestershire sauce or tomato ketchup

3 eggs

3 tbsp plain flour

175 g/6 oz fresh breadcrumbs

sunflower oil, for shallow-frying

✳ salt and pepper

Cabbage Rolls

1. Preheat the oven to 190°C/375°F/Gas Mark 5. Brush a large ovenproof dish with oil.

2. Bring a large saucepan of water to the boil. Add the cabbage leaves, bring back to the boil and blanch for 1 minute. Remove with tongs and drain on kitchen paper.

3. Put the spring onions, garlic, beef and sage into a bowl, season to taste with salt and pepper and mix well until thoroughly combined.

4. Divide the meat mixture into 12 equal-sized portions and shape each into a sausage shape. Place one portion on the stalk end of a cabbage leaf and roll up, tucking in the sides. Put the roll, seam-side down, into the prepared dish. Repeat with the remaining meat mixture and cabbage leaves, arranging them in a single layer in the dish.

5. Sprinkle the sugar evenly over the cabbage rolls and pour the tomatoes, with the can juices, over the top. Cover with foil and bake in the preheated oven for 1 hour, until tender. Serve immediately.

Serves 4–6

olive oil, for brushing

12 large green cabbage leaves, coarse stalks removed

4 spring onions, finely chopped

1 garlic clove, finely chopped

350 g/12 oz fresh beef mince

1 fresh sage sprig, finely chopped

2 tbsp dark brown sugar

400 g/14 oz canned chopped tomatoes

salt and pepper

20

Stuffed Onions

1. Cut a thin slice from the base of the onions and make a circular cut around the top of each. Add the onions to a saucepan of salted boiling water, cover and simmer for 20 minutes. Meanwhile, place the bread in a heatproof bowl with the milk and leave to soak.

2. Remove the onions from the pan using a slotted spoon. Stir the concentrated stock into the cooking liquid and set aside. When the onions are cool enough to handle, scoop out the flesh from the centres without piercing the 'shells'.

3. Squeeze out the bread and put it into a bowl with the beef, garlic, cumin, coriander, 1 tablespoon of the cooking liquid and about three quarters of the beaten egg. Season to taste with salt and pepper and mix well. Using a teaspoon, fill the scooped-out onions with the mixture. Brush the tops with the remaining beaten egg and dust all over with flour.

4. Preheat the oven to 180°C/350°F/Gas Mark 4. Meanwhile, heat enough oil for deep-frying in a deep-fat fryer to 180–190°C/350–375°F, or until a cube of bread browns in 30 seconds. Add the stuffed onions, in batches if necessary, and cook for 5–8 minutes, until evenly browned. Heat the 2 tablespoons of oil in a casserole. Put the onions into the casserole in a single layer and ladle in enough of the cooking liquid to come about halfway up them. Cover and bake in the preheated oven for 30 minutes, until tender. Serve immediately.

Serves 6

12 small onions, peeled

2 slices white bread, crusts removed, halved

175 ml/6 fl oz hot milk

2 tbsp concentrated beef stock or 1 beef stock cube

✳ 280 g/10 oz fresh beef mince

✳ 1 small garlic clove, finely chopped

½ tsp ground cumin

½ tsp ground coriander

2 eggs, lightly beaten

plain flour, for dusting

2 tbsp sunflower oil, plus extra for deep-frying

✳ salt and pepper

21

Meaty Muffins

1. Preheat the oven to 200°C/400°F/Gas Mark 6. Generously grease a 12-cup muffin tin with butter.

2. Put the beef, onion, sweetcorn and parsley into a bowl, season to taste with salt and pepper and mix well until thoroughly combined.

3. Sift the flour, baking powder and a pinch of salt into a separate bowl and make a well in the centre. Lightly beat the eggs with the milk and oil in another bowl, then pour into the well and gradually incorporate the dry ingredients until thoroughly combined.

4. Spoon a little of the muffin mixture into each muffin hole until about a quarter full. Divide the beef mixture among the muffin holes and sprinkle with half the cheese. Top with the remaining muffin mixture and sprinkle with the remaining cheese. Bake in the preheated oven for 20 minutes, until the muffins are golden and the tops spring back when lightly pressed. Serve hot or warm.

Makes 12

butter, for greasing

* 350 g/12 oz fresh beef mince

* 1 small onion, very finely chopped

140 g/5 oz canned sweetcorn, drained

1 tbsp chopped fresh parsley

250 g/9 oz plain flour

2 tsp baking powder

2 eggs

250 ml/9 fl oz milk

125 ml/4 fl oz sunflower oil

115 g/4 oz Cheddar cheese, grated

* salt and pepper

Favourite

22

American Meatballs

1. Tear the bread into pieces, put it into a bowl and pour in enough water to cover. Leave to soak for 5 minutes.

2. Put the beef, onion, tomato ketchup and egg into a bowl and season to taste with salt and pepper. Squeeze out the bread, add it to the bowl and mix well with your hands until thoroughly combined and smooth. Add the 3 tablespoons of water and knead for 5 minutes. Set aside while you make the sauce.

3. For the tomato sauce, heat the oil in a saucepan. Add the onion and garlic and cook over a low heat, stirring occasionally, for 5 minutes, until softened. Meanwhile, mix the tomato purée with the 100 ml/3½ fl oz of water in a small bowl. Add to the saucepan with the tomatoes and bring to the boil, then simmer, stirring occasionally, for 15–20 minutes, until thickened. Transfer the sauce to a food processor or blender and process to a purée. Pour into a clean pan and stir in the sugar to taste.

4. Meanwhile, shape the beef mixture into 20 small meatballs, rolling them between the palms of your hands.

5. Bring the sauce back to a simmer, then add the meatballs and simmer gently, occasionally shaking the pan, for 30 minutes, until cooked through. Garnish with parsley and serve immediately.

Serves 4

3 slices white bread, crusts removed

✳ 650 g/1 lb 7 oz fresh beef mince

✳ 1 onion, grated

125 ml/4 fl oz tomato ketchup

1 egg, lightly beaten

3 tbsp water

✳ salt and pepper

chopped fresh parsley, to garnish

Tomato sauce

2 tbsp sunflower oil

1 onion, finely chopped

2 garlic cloves, finely chopped

2 tbsp tomato purée

100 ml/3½ fl oz water

400 g/14 oz canned chopped tomatoes

1–2 tsp brown sugar

23

Swedish Meatballs

1. Cook the potatoes in a saucepan of salted boiling water for 20–25 minutes, until tender but not falling apart. Drain, tip into a bowl, mash well and leave to cool slightly.

2. Add the fresh breadcrumbs, beef, onion, egg, sugar and spices to the bowl. Season to taste with salt and pepper and mix well until thoroughly combined. Shape the mixture into walnut-sized balls, rolling them between the palms of your hands. Roll the meatballs in the dry breadcrumbs until thoroughly coated.

3. Melt the butter in a large frying pan. Add the meatballs, in batches, and cook over a medium heat, stirring and turning occasionally, for 10 minutes, until golden brown all over and cooked through. Remove with a slotted spoon, drain on kitchen paper and keep warm while you cook the remaining meatballs.

4. When all the meatballs have been cooked, keep them warm while you make the sauce. Stir the flour into the frying pan and cook, stirring constantly, for 1 minute. Remove the pan from the heat and gradually stir in the stock, then add the cream. Season to taste with salt and pepper, return the pan to a low heat and cook, stirring constantly, until thickened and smooth.

5. Return the meatballs to the pan and simmer for 10 minutes. Serve immediately.

Serves 4

2 potatoes, cut into chunks

25 g/1 oz fresh breadcrumbs

650 g/1 lb 7 oz fresh beef mince

1 small onion, grated

1 egg, lightly beaten

1 tsp brown sugar

pinch of each grated nutmeg, ground allspice, ground ginger and ground cloves

55 g/2 oz fine dry breadcrumbs

85 g/3 oz butter

salt and pepper

Sauce
2 tbsp plain flour

225 ml/8 fl oz beef stock

225 ml/8 fl oz double cream

salt and pepper

24

Meatloaf

1. Preheat the oven to 160°C/325°F/Gas Mark 3. Put the beef, onion, garlic (if using), mushrooms, breadcrumbs, eggs, mustard, Worcestershire sauce, celery salt and parsley into a bowl. Season to taste with pepper and mix well until thoroughly combined.

2. Spoon the mixture into a 900-g/2-lb loaf tin, pressing it down well. Cover with the bacon.

3. Put the loaf tin into a roasting tin and pour in boiling water to come about halfway up the sides. Bake in the preheated oven for 1½ hours, until a wooden cocktail stick inserted into the centre comes out clean.

4. Remove the tin from the oven and pour off any fat. Leave to cool for 1 hour. Run a round-bladed knife around the sides of the tin and turn out onto a plate. Wrap the meatloaf in foil and chill in the refrigerator for 4 hours, or overnight. Cut into slices and serve with the tomato sauce.

Serves 4

* 500 g/1 lb 2 oz fresh beef mince
* 1 onion, finely chopped
* 2 garlic cloves, finely chopped (optional)
  115 g/4 oz mushrooms, finely chopped
  85 g/3 oz fresh breadcrumbs
  2 eggs, lightly beaten
  2 tsp Dijon mustard
  1 tsp Worcestershire sauce
  1 tsp celery salt
  1 tbsp chopped fresh parsley
  8–10 streaky bacon rashers
* pepper
  1 quantity Tomato Sauce (see page 58), to serve

Spaghetti Bolognese

1. Heat the oil in a saucepan. Add the pancetta, onion, carrot, celery and garlic and cook over a low heat, stirring occasionally, for 5 minutes, until softened.

2. Add the beef, increase the heat to medium and cook, stirring frequently and breaking up the meat with a wooden spoon, for 8–10 minutes, until evenly browned. Stir in the mushrooms and chicken livers, if using, and cook, stirring frequently, for a further 3–4 minutes.

3. Stir in the tomatoes, tomato purée, wine, stock, bay leaf and oregano. Season to taste with salt and pepper, then bring to the boil. Reduce the heat, cover and simmer, stirring occasionally, for 1 hour.

4. When the sauce is nearly ready, bring a saucepan of salted water to the boil. Add the spaghetti, return to the boil and cook for 8–10 minutes, until tender but still firm to the bite. Drain the pasta, return it to the pan and toss with the butter.

5. Remove the sauce from the heat and discard the bay leaf. Add the spaghetti and toss well, then transfer to a warmed serving dish. Sprinkle with Parmesan cheese shavings and serve immediately.

Serves 4

2 tbsp olive oil

85 g/3 oz pancetta or bacon, diced

1 onion, finely chopped

1 carrot, finely chopped

1 celery stick, finely chopped

2 garlic cloves, finely chopped

500 g/1 lb 2 oz fresh beef mince

115 g/4 oz mushrooms, thinly sliced

115 g/4 oz chicken livers, finely chopped (optional)

400 g/14 oz canned chopped tomatoes

2 tbsp tomato purée

150 ml/5 fl oz white wine

300 ml/10 fl oz beef stock

1 bay leaf

pinch of dried oregano

450 g/1 lb dried spaghetti

25 g/1 oz butter

salt and pepper

Parmesan cheese shavings, to serve

26

Meaty Macaroni Cheese

1. Heat the oil in a saucepan. Add the onion and garlic and cook over a low heat, stirring occasionally, for 5 minutes, until softened. Add the beef, increase the heat to medium and cook, breaking it up with a wooden spoon, for 8–10 minutes, until lightly browned all over. Stir in the sweetcorn, tomatoes and mixed herbs and season to taste with salt and pepper. Reduce the heat, cover and simmer, stirring occasionally, for 25–30 minutes.

2. Bring a large pan of salted water to the boil. Add the macaroni, return to the boil and cook for 10 minutes, until tender but still firm to the bite.

3. Meanwhile, preheat the grill. Melt the butter in a separate saucepan. Sprinkle in the flour and cook, stirring constantly, for 2 minutes. Remove the pan from the heat and gradually stir in the milk, a little at a time. Return the pan to the heat and bring to the boil, stirring constantly. Reduce the heat and simmer the sauce, stirring constantly, for 5 minutes, until thickened and smooth. Remove the pan from the heat and stir in the mustard and 150 g/5½ oz of the cheese. Stir well until the cheese has melted.

4. Drain the macaroni and tip it into the cheese sauce, stirring well to mix. Spoon the beef mixture into a baking dish, then cover with the macaroni mixture. Sprinkle with the remaining cheese and cook under the preheated grill for 4–5 minutes, until the top is golden and bubbling. Serve immediately.

Serves 6

2 tbsp olive oil

* 1 onion, chopped
* 1 garlic clove, finely chopped
* 500 g/1 lb 2 oz fresh beef mince

200 g/7 oz canned sweetcorn, drained

400 g/14 oz canned chopped tomatoes

1 tsp dried mixed herbs

225 g/8 oz dried macaroni

40 g/1½ oz butter

40 g/1½ oz plain flour

500 ml/18 fl oz milk

2 tsp Dijon mustard

200 g/7 oz Cheddar cheese, grated

* salt and pepper

Spaghetti & Meatballs

1. Heat the oil in a frying pan. Add the chopped onion and garlic and cook over a low heat, for 5 minutes, until softened. Remove from the heat and tip the mixture into a bowl with the thyme, beef, breadcrumbs and egg. Season to taste with salt and pepper and mix well. Shape into 20 meatballs.

2. Heat a large non-stick frying pan over a low–medium heat. Add the meatballs and cook, stirring gently and turning frequently, for 15 minutes, until lightly browned all over.

3. Meanwhile, preheat the grill. Put the onion wedges and pepper halves, skin-side up, on a grill rack and cook under the preheated grill, turning frequently, for 10 minutes, until the pepper skins are blistered and charred. Put the peppers into a plastic bag, tie the top and leave to cool. Set the onion wedges aside.

4. Peel off the pepper skins. Roughly chop the flesh and put it into a food processor or blender with the onion wedges and tomatoes. Process to a smooth purée and season to taste with salt and pepper. Pour into a saucepan with the bay leaf and bring to the boil. Reduce the heat and simmer, stirring occasionally, for 10 minutes. Remove and discard the bay leaf.

5. Meanwhile, bring a saucepan of salted water to the boil. Add the spaghetti, return to the boil and cook for 8–10 minutes, until tender but still firm to the bite. Drain the spaghetti and serve immediately with the meatballs and sauce.

Serves 4

1 tbsp olive oil

1 small onion, finely chopped

2 garlic cloves, finely chopped

2 fresh thyme sprigs, finely chopped

650 g/1 lb 7 oz fresh beef mince

25 g/1 oz fresh breadcrumbs

1 egg, lightly beaten

450 g/1 lb dried spaghetti

salt and pepper

Sauce

1 onion, cut into wedges

3 red peppers, halved and deseeded

400 g/14 oz canned chopped tomatoes

1 bay leaf

salt and pepper

Classic Lasagne

1. Heat the oil in a saucepan. Add the bacon and cook, stirring frequently, for 3–4 minutes. Add the onion, garlic, carrots and celery and cook over a low heat, stirring occasionally, for 5 minutes, until softened. Add the beef, increase the heat to medium and cook, stirring frequently and breaking it up with a wooden spoon, for 8–10 minutes, until evenly browned. Stir in the oregano, parsley and tomatoes. Season to taste with salt and pepper, then reduce the heat and simmer, stirring occasionally, for 30 minutes.

2. Preheat the oven to 200°C/400°F/Gas Mark 6. Meanwhile, make the Béchamel sauce. Pour the milk into a saucepan and add the peppercorns, onion, bay leaf and mace. Bring to the boil, then remove from the heat and leave to infuse for 10 minutes. Strain the milk into a jug and discard the flavourings. Melt the butter in a separate saucepan. Stir in the flour and cook, stirring constantly, for 2 minutes. Gradually stir in the flavoured milk, a little at a time, and bring to the boil, stirring constantly. Reduce the heat and simmer, stirring constantly for a few minutes, until thickened and smooth. Remove from the heat and season to taste with salt and pepper.

3. Make alternating layers of the beef mixture, lasagne sheets, Béchamel sauce and Parmesan in an ovenproof dish, ending with a layer of Béchamel sauce sprinkled with Parmesan. Bake in the preheated oven for 30 minutes, until golden brown. Leave to stand for 10 minutes before serving.

Serves 6

3 tbsp olive oil

2 bacon rashers, chopped

1 Spanish onion, chopped

2 garlic cloves, finely chopped

2 carrots, chopped

2 celery sticks, chopped

350 g/12 oz fresh beef mince

pinch of dried oregano

1 tbsp chopped fresh parsley

400 g/14 oz canned chopped tomatoes

225 g/8 oz no pre-cook lasagne sheets

115 g/4 oz Parmesan cheese, grated

salt and pepper

Béchamel sauce

500 ml/18 fl oz milk

6 black peppercorns

1 slice onion

1 bay leaf

1 mace blade

55 g/2 oz butter

55 g/2 oz plain flour

salt and pepper

29

Sloppy Joes

1. Put the beef, onion, garlic and green pepper into a non-stick frying pan and cook over a medium heat, stirring frequently and breaking up the beef with a wooden spoon, for 8–10 minutes, until the beef is evenly browned. Carefully drain off the fat.

2. Stir in the mustard, tomato ketchup, vinegar, brown sugar and chilli powder, if using. Season to taste with salt and pepper. Reduce the heat and simmer, stirring occasionally, for 30 minutes.

3. Divide the mixture among the burger buns and serve immediately.

Serves 4

* 450 g/1 lb fresh beef mince
* 1 onion, chopped
* 1 garlic clove, chopped
* 1 green pepper, deseeded and chopped
* 1 tbsp American mustard
* 175 ml/6 fl oz tomato ketchup
* 1 tsp white vinegar
* 1 tbsp brown sugar
* pinch of chilli powder, ground cloves or paprika (optional)
* 4 burger buns, split
* salt and pepper

Cheese-stuffed Burgers

1. Preheat the grill. Put the beef, onion, garlic, horseradish and thyme into a bowl. Season to taste with salt and pepper and mix well until thoroughly combined. Divide the mixture into eight portions and shape each portion into a patty shape.

2. Sprinkle the cheese over four of the patties and top with the remaining patties. Gently press the edges together, smoothing them with a palette knife to enclose the cheese completely.

3. Cook under the preheated grill for 5–6 minutes on each side, turning them carefully with a fish slice. Serve in the toasted buns with rocket leaves.

Serves 4

* 500 g/1 lb 2 oz fresh beef mince
* 1 onion, finely chopped
* 1 garlic clove, finely chopped
  1 tsp creamed horseradish
  1 tbsp chopped fresh thyme
  55 g/2 oz Gorgonzola, Lancashire or feta cheese, crumbled
  4 burger buns, split and toasted
* salt and pepper
  rocket leaves, to serve

Stuffed Peppers

1. Cut off the tops of the peppers and remove the seeds and membranes without piercing the 'shells', then set aside. Cut out the stems from the sliced tops and chop the flesh.

2. Heat the oil in a frying pan. Add the onions, garlic, chillies and chopped pepper and cook over a low heat, stirring occasionally, for 5 minutes, until softened. Add the beef and Tabasco and season to taste with salt. Increase the heat to medium and cook, stirring frequently and breaking up the meat with a wooden spoon, for 8–10 minutes, until evenly browned. Stir in the flour, then gradually stir in the stock. Bring to the boil, stirring constantly, then reduce the heat, cover and simmer for 30 minutes.

3. Preheat the oven to 180°C/350°F/Gas Mark 4. Brush an ovenproof dish with oil. Remove the frying pan from the heat and spoon the beef mixture into the peppers. Stand them upright in the prepared dish and bake in the preheated oven for 45 minutes.

4. Put the cream, cream cheese and cayenne pepper into a saucepan, season to taste with salt and stir until smooth. Add the sultanas and cook over a medium heat, stirring constantly, until hot. Do not allow the mixture to boil.

5. Remove the peppers from the oven and pour the cream cheese sauce over them. Return to the oven and bake for a further 15 minutes. Serve immediately.

Serves 4

4 large red peppers

3 tbsp sunflower oil, plus extra for brushing

2 onions, finely chopped

2 garlic cloves, finely chopped

2 fresh green chillies, deseeded and finely chopped

500 g/1 lb 2 oz fresh beef mince

1 tsp Tabasco sauce

2 tbsp plain flour

225 ml/8 fl oz beef stock

150 ml/5 fl oz single cream

225 g/8 oz cream cheese

pinch of cayenne pepper

115 g/4 oz sultanas

salt

32

Family Mince & Mash

1. Heat the oil in a frying pan. Add the onion and carrots and cook over a low heat, stirring occasionally, for 5 minutes, until softened. Add the beef, increase the heat to medium and cook, stirring frequently and breaking it up with a wooden spoon, for 8–10 minutes, until evenly browned.

2. Stir in the thyme and oats, then pour in the stock. Season to taste with salt and pepper and bring to the boil. Reduce the heat, cover and simmer, stirring occasionally, for 25–30 minutes, until thickened.

3. Meanwhile, cook the parsnips and potatoes in a large saucepan of salted boiling water for 10–15 minutes, until tender but not falling apart. Remove from the heat and drain. Return the vegetables to the pan and add the butter and cream. Season to taste with salt and pepper, then mash well until smooth.

4. Divide the mash among individual plates. Top with the beef mixture, garnish with parsley sprigs and serve immediately.

Serves 6

2 tbsp sunflower oil

1 onion, finely chopped

2 carrots, finely chopped

1 kg/2 lb 4 oz fresh beef mince

1 tbsp chopped fresh thyme

2 tbsp rolled oats

225 ml/8 fl oz beef stock

1 kg/2 lb 4 oz parsnips, finely chopped

1 kg/2 lb 4 oz potatoes, finely chopped

115 g/4 oz butter

6 tbsp double cream

salt and pepper

fresh flat-leaf parsley sprigs, to garnish

Stuffed Baked Potatoes

1. Preheat the oven to 220°C/425°F/Gas Mark 7. Prick the potatoes all over with a fork. Put them directly on an oven shelf and bake in the preheated oven for 1¼–1½ hours, until soft.

2. Meanwhile, heat the oil in a large saucepan. Add the bacon and cook over a low heat, stirring occasionally, for 5 minutes. Add the onion, garlic and celery and cook, stirring occasionally, for 5 minutes, until softened.

3. Add the beef, increase the heat to medium and cook, stirring frequently and breaking it up with a wooden spoon, for 8–10 minutes, until evenly browned. Add the tomatoes, tomato ketchup, Worcestershire sauce, sage and thyme. Season to taste with salt and pepper. Reduce the heat, cover and simmer, stirring occasionally, for 30 minutes.

4. Remove the potatoes from the oven and reduce the oven temperature to 190°C/375°F/Gas Mark 5. Halve the potatoes and carefully scoop out the flesh into a bowl. Spoon the beef mixture into the potato shells to half-fill them. Mash the scooped-out potato with the butter and cheese, then spoon it into the potato shells on top of the beef mixture. Put the potatoes into an ovenproof dish and bake for 15–20 minutes. Serve immediately.

Serves 4

4 large baking potatoes

2 tbsp sunflower oil

4 bacon rashers, finely chopped

1 onion, finely chopped

1 garlic clove, finely chopped

1 celery stick, finely chopped

450 g/1 lb fresh beef mince

400 g/14 oz canned chopped tomatoes

1 tbsp tomato ketchup

1 tbsp Worcestershire sauce

1 tsp chopped fresh sage

1 tsp chopped fresh thyme

85 g/3 oz butter

85 g/3 oz feta cheese, crumbled

salt and pepper

34

Minced Beef Pizza

1. Preheat the oven to 200°C/400°F/Gas Mark 6. Brush a baking sheet with oil. To make the pizza dough, sift the flour and salt into a bowl. Add the butter and rub it in with your fingertips until the mixture resembles breadcrumbs. Pour in 100 ml/3½ fl oz of the milk and mix with a round-bladed knife to a soft dough, adding the remaining milk if necessary.

2. Turn out the dough onto a lightly floured surface and knead gently. Roll out to a 25-cm/10-inch round and transfer to the prepared baking sheet. Push up the edge slightly all around to make a rim.

3. Put the beef, onion, garlic and cumin in a non-stick frying pan and cook over a medium heat, stirring frequently and breaking up the meat with a wooden spoon, for 5–8 minutes, until evenly browned. Stir in the red pepper and coriander and season to taste with salt and pepper.

4. Spread the tomato purée over the pizza base. Cover with the beef mixture, top with the mozzarella and drizzle with oil. Bake in the preheated oven for 15–20 minutes, until the crust is crisp. Serve immediately.

Serves 2

olive oil, for brushing and drizzling

* 175 g/6 oz fresh beef mince
* 1 small onion, finely chopped
* 1 garlic clove, finely chopped
* 1 tsp ground cumin
55 g/2 oz chargrilled red pepper in oil, drained and finely chopped
1 tbsp chopped fresh coriander
4 tbsp tomato purée
115 g/4 oz mozzarella cheese, sliced
* salt and pepper

Pizza dough
175 g/6 oz self-raising flour, plus extra for dusting
pinch of salt
25 g/1 oz butter, cut into small pieces
100–125 ml/3½–4 fl oz milk

35

Beef in Pitta Pockets

1. Heat the oil in a frying pan. Add the onion and garlic and cook over a low heat, stirring occasionally, for 5 minutes, until softened. Add the beef, increase the heat to medium and cook, stirring frequently and breaking it up with a wooden spoon, for 8–10 minutes, until evenly browned. Stir in the tomatoes, cumin, ground coriander and turmeric. Season to taste with salt and pepper, reduce the heat and simmer, stirring occasionally, for 15–20 minutes.

2. Meanwhile, dry-fry the pine kernels in a small frying pan, stirring constantly, until golden. Stir the pine kernels and chopped coriander into the meat mixture and simmer for 3–4 minutes.

3. To serve, cut a slit in the side of each pitta bread to make a pocket. Put a little of the beef mixture into each pocket with some chopped cucumber and shredded lettuce. Top with a spoonful of soured cream and serve immediately.

Serves 4

2 tbsp olive oil

* 1 onion, chopped
* 1 garlic clove, chopped
* 500 g/1 lb 2 oz fresh beef mince

200 g/7 oz canned chopped tomatoes

1 tsp ground cumin

1 tsp ground coriander

½ tsp ground turmeric

85 g/3 oz pine kernels

2 tbsp chopped fresh coriander

* salt and pepper

To serve
8 pitta breads, warmed
chopped cucumber
shredded lettuce
soured cream

Beef 'n' Beans

1. Put the onion and beef into a large non-stick frying pan and cook over a medium heat, stirring frequently and breaking up the meat with a wooden spoon, for 8–10 minutes, until evenly browned.

2. Stir the baked beans, maple syrup, mustard and concentrated stock into the frying pan and season to taste with pepper. Reduce the heat, cover and simmer, stirring occasionally and adding a little water if the mixture seems to be drying out, for 15 minutes.

3. Meanwhile, cook the potatoes in a saucepan of salted boiling water for 20 minutes, until tender but not falling apart. Drain the potatoes and return to the pan. Add the cream cheese, season to taste with salt and pepper and mash until smooth.

4. Preheat the grill. Transfer the beef mixture to an ovenproof dish and spread the mashed potato over the top. Cook under the preheated grill for 5 minutes, until the topping is golden brown. Serve immediately.

Serves 4

✳ 1 onion, chopped
✳ 500 g/1 lb 2 oz fresh beef mince
400 g/14 oz canned baked beans
1 tbsp maple syrup
1 tbsp mild mustard
1 tbsp concentrated beef stock
650 g/1 lb 7 oz potatoes, diced
115 g/4 oz cream cheese
✳ salt and pepper

Minced Beef Hash

1. Cook the potatoes in a saucepan of salted boiling water for 20–25 minutes, until tender but not falling apart. Drain and leave to cool.

2. Meanwhile, mix together the beef, red pepper, paprika and parsley in a bowl. Season to taste with salt and pepper. Dice the potatoes and add them to the mixture, stirring gently until thoroughly combined.

3. Heat the oil in a large frying pan. Add the onion and cook over a low heat, stirring occasionally, for 5 minutes, until softened.

4. Add the beef mixture to the pan and shake the pan to mix it with the onion, then press down gently with a wooden spoon. Cook over a medium heat, without stirring, for 5 minutes, until browned on the underside. Stir well, then cook, without stirring, for 5 minutes. Repeat the stirring and cooking twice more until the mixture is evenly browned.

5. Reduce the heat. Make two hollows in the mixture with the back of a spoon. Crack an egg into each hollow, cover and cook for a further 5 minutes, until the whites have set. Cut the hash into halves, each containing an egg, garnish with parsley and serve immediately.

Serves 2

450 g/1 lb potatoes, cut into chunks

350 g/12 oz fresh beef mince

1 red pepper, deseeded and finely chopped

½ tsp sweet paprika

1 tbsp chopped fresh parsley, plus extra to garnish

3 tbsp sunflower oil

1 onion, finely chopped

2 eggs

salt and pepper

38

Simple Savoury Beef

1 · Melt the butter in a saucepan. Add the onion and carrots and cook over a low heat, stirring occasionally, for 5 minutes, until softened. Add the tomatoes and cook, stirring occasionally, for a further 3 minutes.

2 Remove the pan from the heat and stir in the flour and mustard powder, then return to the heat and cook, stirring constantly, for 2 minutes. Gradually stir in the stock, a little at a time, then bring to the boil, stirring constantly. Cook, stirring constantly, for a further few minutes, until thickened.

3 Add the beef and stir to break it up. Season to taste with salt and pepper, then cover and simmer, stirring occasionally, for 45 minutes.

4 Gently stir in the peas, re-cover the pan and simmer, stirring occasionally, for a further 15 minutes. Taste and adjust the seasoning, adding salt and pepper if needed. Garnish with parsley and serve immediately.

Serves 4

55 g/2 oz butter

✳ 1 Spanish onion, finely chopped

2 carrots, finely chopped

4 tomatoes, peeled and chopped

25 g/1 oz plain flour

1 tsp mustard powder

600 ml/1 pint beef stock

✳ 500 g/1 lb 2 oz fresh beef mince

175 g/6 oz frozen peas

✳ salt and pepper

chopped fresh parsley, to garnish

39

Salisbury Steak

1. Put the onion, breadcrumbs and egg into a bowl and mix well. Mix together the undiluted soup, horseradish, Worcestershire sauce and mustard in a separate bowl, stirring until thoroughly combined.

2. Add 4 tablespoons of the soup mixture to the onion mixture, then stir in the beef and season to taste with salt and pepper. Mix well until thoroughly combined. Divide the mixture into six portions and shape them into patties.

3. Heat the oil in a large frying pan. Add the patties and cook over a medium heat for 3–4 minutes on each side, until lightly browned.

4. Stir the stock into the remaining soup mixture and pour it into the pan. Reduce the heat, cover and simmer for 12–15 minutes, until the patties are cooked through. Garnish with parsley and serve immediately.

Serves 6

* 1 small onion, finely chopped
25 g/1 oz dry breadcrumbs
1 egg, lightly beaten
300 ml/10 fl oz canned condensed cream of mushroom soup
1 tsp creamed horseradish
1 tbsp Worcestershire sauce
1 tbsp Dijon mustard
* 700 g/1 lb 9 oz fresh beef mince
2 tbsp sunflower oil
125 ml/4 fl oz beef stock
* salt and pepper
chopped fresh parsley, to garnish

Comforting

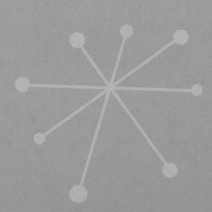

40

Tamale Pie

1. Preheat the oven to 190°C/375°F/Gas Mark 5. Heat the oil in a large frying pan. Add the onion and cook over a low heat, stirring occasionally, for 5 minutes, until softened.

2. Add the beef, increase the heat to medium and cook, stirring frequently and breaking it up with a wooden spoon, for 8–10 minutes, until evenly browned. Stir in the chilli powder, tomatoes, sweetcorn, olives and soured cream and season to taste with salt, then transfer the mixture to an ovenproof dish.

3. Put the cornmeal, baking powder, butter and milk in a food processor and process until combined. With the motor running, gradually add enough of the hot stock through the feeder tube to make a thick, smooth mixture.

4. Pour the cornmeal mixture over the beef mixture and smooth the surface with a palette knife. Bake in the preheated oven for 20 minutes, until the topping is just beginning to brown. Sprinkle with the cheese, return to the oven and bake for a further 15 minutes, until golden and bubbling. Serve immediately.

Serves 6

2 tbsp corn oil

✳ 1 onion, finely chopped

✳ 350 g/12 oz fresh beef mince

1½ tsp chilli powder

200 g/7 oz canned chopped tomatoes

140 g/5 oz canned sweetcorn, drained

2 tbsp chopped stoned black olives

100 ml/3½ fl oz soured cream

125 g/4½ oz cornmeal or coarse polenta

½ tsp baking powder

55 g/2 oz butter, cut into pieces

3 tbsp milk

about 225 ml/8 fl oz hot chicken stock

85 g/3 oz Cheddar cheese, grated

✳ salt

41

Cottage Pie

1. Cook the potatoes in a large saucepan of salted boiling water for 20–25 minutes, until tender but not falling apart.

2. Meanwhile, heat the oil in a saucepan. Add the onion, garlic (if using) and carrots and cook over a low heat, stirring occasionally, for 5 minutes, until the onion has softened. Increase the heat to medium, add the beef and cook, stirring frequently and breaking it up with a wooden spoon, for 8–10 minutes, until evenly browned.

3. Add the mushrooms and cook for 2 minutes, then pour in the stock and stir in the sugar and Worcestershire sauce. Season to taste with salt and pepper. Reduce the heat, cover and simmer for 20 minutes.

4. Preheat the oven to 200°C/400°F/Gas Mark 6. Drain the potatoes, return to the pan and mash well, then stir in three quarters of the cheese.

5. Spoon the meat mixture into an ovenproof dish and spread the mashed potato over the top to cover. Sprinkle with the remaining cheese and bake in the preheated oven for 20 minutes, until the topping is golden brown. Serve immediately.

Serves 6

650 g/1 lb 7 oz potatoes, cut into chunks

2 tbsp sunflower oil

1 onion, chopped

1 garlic clove, chopped (optional)

2 carrots, chopped

500 g/1 lb 2 oz fresh beef mince

115 g/4 oz mushrooms, sliced

300 ml/10 fl oz hot beef stock

1 tsp sugar

1 tbsp Worcestershire sauce

115 g/4 oz Cheddar cheese, grated

salt and pepper

Beef with Garlic Potatoes

1. Preheat the oven to 180°C/350°F/Gas Mark 4. Parboil the potatoes in a saucepan of salted boiling water for 15 minutes, then drain and leave to cool.

2. Meanwhile, heat 1 tablespoon of the oil in a large saucepan. Add the onion and cook over a low heat, stirring occasionally, for 5 minutes, until softened.

3. Add the beef, increase the heat to medium and cook, stirring frequently and breaking it up with a wooden spoon, for 8–10 minutes, until evenly browned. Add the carrots and tomatoes. Stir the cornflour into the stock, then stir the mixture into the pan. Season to taste with salt and pepper. Stir in the parsley and sage and bring to the boil, then reduce the heat and simmer for 5 minutes.

4. Meanwhile, cut the potatoes into slices. Mix together the garlic and the remaining oil in a small bowl and season to taste with salt and pepper.

5. Transfer the beef mixture to an ovenproof dish and arrange the potato slices on top. Brush the garlic-flavoured oil over them and bake in the preheated oven for 30–35 minutes, until the topping is golden brown. Serve immediately.

Serves 4

500 g/1 lb 2 oz potatoes

3 tbsp olive oil

1 onion, chopped

500 g/1 lb 2 oz fresh beef mince

225 g/8 oz carrots, chopped

4 tomatoes, peeled and chopped

1 tsp cornflour

300 ml/10 fl oz hot beef stock

1 tbsp chopped fresh parsley

1 tsp chopped fresh sage

3 garlic cloves, very finely chopped

salt and pepper

Minced Beef Casserole

1. Heat 2 tablespoons of the oil in a large frying pan. Add the beef and cook over a medium heat, stirring frequently and breaking it up with a wooden spoon, for 8 minutes, until lightly browned. Stir in the spring onions, tomatoes, red pepper and pineapple and cook, stirring occasionally, for a further 5 minutes. Stir in the thyme and season to taste with salt and pepper. Reduce the heat and simmer, stirring occasionally, for 15 minutes.

2. Preheat the oven to 180°C/350°F/Gas Mark 4. Heat the remaining oil in a frying pan. Add the aubergine slices, in batches, and cook for 2–3 minutes on each side, until softened. Add more oil to the pan as required. Remove the aubergine slices from the pan and drain on kitchen paper.

3. Put one third of the aubergine slices in an ovenproof dish and add half the beef mixture. Add half the remaining aubergine slices and top with the remaining beef mixture. Cover with the remaining aubergine slices, sprinkle with the cheese and bake in the preheated oven for 30 minutes, until the topping is golden brown. Serve immediately.

Serves 6

6 tbsp olive oil, plus extra if needed

1 kg/2 lb 4 oz fresh beef mince

6 spring onions, chopped

6 tomatoes, peeled and chopped

1 red pepper, deseeded and sliced

2 slices fresh pineapple (about 2 cm/¾ inch thick), peeled, cored and chopped

1 tbsp chopped fresh thyme

2 aubergines, thinly sliced

175 g/6 oz Cheddar cheese, grated

salt and pepper

44

Braised Beef Burgers

1. Put the beef, garlic, shallot, celery, breadcrumbs, basil and egg into a bowl and season to taste with salt and pepper. Mix well until thoroughly combined, then divide the mixture into four equal portions and shape them into patties.

2. Heat the oil in a frying pan. Add the burgers and cook over a medium heat for 3 minutes on each side, until browned. Remove from the pan and keep warm.

3. Add the onion to the pan and cook over a low heat, stirring occasionally, for 5 minutes, until softened. Drain off as much fat as possible. Return the pan to the heat and stir in the stock, then add the bay leaf and season to taste with salt. Return the burgers to the pan and simmer gently for 25 minutes.

4. Transfer the burgers to warmed individual plates. Remove and discard the bay leaf, then pour the sauce over the burgers and serve immediately.

Serves 4

* 650 g/1 lb 7 oz fresh beef mince
* 2 garlic cloves, finely chopped
* 1 shallot, finely chopped
1 celery stick, finely chopped
25 g/1 oz fresh breadcrumbs
1 fresh basil sprig, finely chopped
1 egg, lightly beaten
2 tbsp sunflower oil
1 small onion, chopped
225 ml/8 fl oz beef stock
1 bay leaf
* salt and pepper

Baked Beef & Potato Layers

1. Mix the tomato purée with the water in a bowl, then add to a saucepan with the tomatoes and thyme. Season to taste with salt and pepper. Bring to the boil, then reduce the heat and simmer, stirring occasionally, for 30 minutes, until thickened.

2. Meanwhile, cook the potatoes in a saucepan of salted boiling water for 20–25 minutes, until tender but not falling apart. Drain and leave to cool slightly, then cut into 5-mm/¼-inch slices.

3. Preheat the oven to 180°C/350°F/Gas Mark 4. Rub the cut sides of the garlic all over an ovenproof dish, then grease the dish with butter.

4. Mix together the beef and egg in a bowl and season to taste with salt and pepper. Divide the mixture into six portions and shape each into a patty about 5 mm/¼ inch thick. Melt 25 g/1 oz of the butter in a frying pan. Add the patties and cook over a medium heat for 3 minutes on each side, until lightly browned. Remove with a fish slice and keep warm. Add the onions to the frying pan and cook over a low heat, stirring occasionally, for 5 minutes, until softened.

5. Put half the potato slices in the base of the prepared dish. Cover with the beef patties, then the onions and sprinkle with half the cheese. Top with the remaining potato slices and pour over the tomato mixture. Sprinkle with the remaining cheese, dot with the remaining butter and bake in the preheated oven for 20 minutes. Serve immediately.

Serves 4

55 g/2 oz tomato purée

125 ml/4 fl oz water

400 g/14 oz canned chopped tomatoes

1 tbsp chopped fresh thyme

500 g/1 lb 2 oz potatoes

1 garlic clove, halved

225 g/8 oz fresh beef mince

1 egg, lightly beaten

40 g/1½ oz butter, plus extra for greasing

2 onions, sliced

115 g/4 oz Cheddar cheese, grated

salt and pepper

Layered Beef & Feta

1. Heat half the oil in a large frying pan. Add the onion and garlic and cook over a low heat, stirring occasionally, for 5 minutes, until softened. Add the beef, increase the heat to medium and cook, stirring frequently and breaking up the meat with a wooden spoon, for 8–10 minutes, until evenly browned. Drain off the fat and return the pan to the heat. Stir in the tomato purée and cook for a further 2–3 minutes, then stir in the tomatoes, Worcestershire sauce and oregano. Season to taste with salt and pepper. Reduce the heat, cover and simmer for 30 minutes.

2. Meanwhile, cook the potatoes in a saucepan of salted boiling water for 20–25 minutes, until tender but not falling apart. Drain and leave to cool slightly, then cut into thick slices.

3. Preheat the oven to 180°C/350°F/Gas Mark 4. Brush the aubergine slices with the remaining oil. Heat a large heavy-based frying pan. Add the aubergine slices, in batches, and cook over a medium heat for 3 minutes on each side, until softened. Drain on kitchen paper.

4. Transfer the beef mixture to an ovenproof dish and cover with the potato slices, followed by the aubergine slices. Crumble the feta over the top. Mix the yogurt, eggs and half the Parmesan in a bowl and pour evenly over the dish. Sprinkle with the remaining Parmesan and bake in the preheated oven for 30–35 minutes, until golden brown. Serve immediately.

Serves 6

4 tbsp olive oil

1 onion, chopped

2 garlic cloves, finely chopped

650 g/1 lb 7 oz fresh beef mince

1½ tbsp tomato purée

600 g/1 lb 5 oz canned chopped tomatoes

2 tbsp Worcestershire sauce

1 tbsp chopped fresh oregano

750 g/1 lb 10 oz potatoes

2 aubergines, sliced

150 g/5½ oz feta cheese

600 ml/1 pint Greek-style yogurt

3 large eggs, lightly beaten

40 g/1½ oz Parmesan cheese, grated

salt and pepper

47

Beef with Pimientos

1. Heat the oil in a large frying pan. Add the onions and garlic and cook over a low heat, stirring occasionally, for 5 minutes, until softened. Add the beef, increase the heat to medium and cook, stirring frequently and breaking up the meat with a wooden spoon, for 8–10 minutes, until evenly browned.

2. Stir in the Worcestershire sauce, lemon juice, paprika and sugar. Season to taste with salt and pepper, then cook, stirring frequently, for 5 minutes. Add the pimientos, reduce the heat and simmer, stirring occasionally, for 20 minutes, until the meat is cooked through and tender. Serve immediately.

Serves 4

2 tbsp olive oil

✳ 3 large onions, thinly sliced into rings

✳ 2 garlic cloves, finely chopped

✳ 650 g/1 lb 7 oz fresh beef mince

2 tbsp Worcestershire sauce

3 tbsp lemon juice

1 tsp hot paprika

1 tbsp light brown sugar

115 g/4 oz canned or bottled pimientos, drained and sliced lengthways

✳ salt and pepper

Salisbury Casserole

1. Line a 38 x 25-cm/15 x 10-inch ovenproof dish with baking paper. Crush the biscuits, put them into a bowl and pour in the water. Leave to soak for 5 minutes, then add the beef and season to taste with salt and pepper. Mix well, then spoon the mixture into the prepared dish, pressing it down well with the back of the spoon. Cover with clingfilm and chill in the refrigerator for 8 hours or overnight.

2. Preheat the oven to 150°C/300°F/Gas Mark 2. Uncover the dish, cut the beef mixture into 12 rectangles and carefully remove from the dish, using the baking paper to help you. Remove and discard the baking paper. Pour the undiluted soup into the dish.

3. Dust the beef rectangles with flour. Heat the oil in a large frying pan. Add the rectangles, in batches, and cook for 3–4 minutes on each side, until lightly browned. Remove with a fish slice and drain on kitchen paper, then return to the dish.

4. Bake in the preheated oven for 40–45 minutes, until the meat is tender. Transfer the rectangles to warmed individual plates, spoon the sauce over them and serve immediately.

Serves 6

225 g/8 oz water biscuits, crackers or matzos

225 ml/8 fl oz water

* 1.3 kg/3 lb fresh beef mince

300 ml/10 fl oz condensed French onion soup

plain flour, for dusting

2 tbsp sunflower oil

* salt and pepper

Fried Beef Dumplings with Tomato Sauce

1. Put the beef, suet and onion into a bowl and mix well. Add the spices, season to taste with salt and pepper and mix well again. Finally, add the egg and mix until thoroughly combined.

2. Break off pieces of the mixture and shape into 5-cm/2-inch balls. Spread out the oatmeal in a shallow dish and roll the dumplings in it until coated.

3. Heat enough oil for deep-frying in a deep-fat fryer to 180–190°C/350–375°F, or until a cube of bread browns in 30 seconds. Add the dumplings and cook for 8–10 minutes, until golden brown and cooked through.

4. Remove the dumplings and drain well. Transfer to a warmed serving dish and serve immediately with the tomato sauce.

Serves 6

* 650 g/1 lb 7 oz fresh beef mince
* 250 g/9 oz shredded beef suet
* 4½ tbsp finely chopped onion
* ½ tsp ground ginger
* ¼ tsp ground cloves
* ¼ tsp ground nutmeg
* 1 large egg, lightly beaten
* 85 g/3 oz medium oatmeal
* vegetable oil, for deep-frying
* salt and pepper
* 1 quantity Tomato Sauce, to serve (see page 58)

50

Beef-filled Crêpes

1. First, make the crêpe batter. Sift the flour and salt into a bowl, then add the egg and half the milk and beat until the mixture is smooth. Stir in the remaining milk and the oil. Set aside.

2. Heat the oil in a frying pan. Add the onion and carrots and cook over a low heat, stirring occasionally, for 5 minutes, until softened. Add the beef, increase the heat to medium and cook, stirring frequently and breaking it up with a wooden spoon, for 8–10 minutes, until evenly browned. Reserve 2 tablespoons of the stock, then stir the tomato purée into the remainder and add to the frying pan. Season to taste with salt and pepper, reduce the heat and simmer, stirring occasionally, for 30 minutes.

3. Meanwhile, brush a 25-cm/10-inch crêpe pan with oil and heat. Stir the batter and pour a little into the centre of the hot pan, then tilt and rotate the pan to cover the base evenly. Cook for 1–1½ minutes, until the underside is golden brown, then flip over the crêpe and cook on the other side for 30 seconds. Make more crêpes with the remaining batter, brushing the pan with more oil as required.

4. Preheat the oven to 190°C/375°F/Gas Mark 5. Mix the flour with the reserved stock and stir into the beef mixture. Simmer, stirring constantly, for a few minutes, until thickened. Divide the beef filling among the crêpes and roll them up. Put them into an ovenproof dish in a single layer and bake in the preheated oven for 15 minutes. Serve immediately.

Serves 4

2 tbsp sunflower oil, plus extra for brushing

1 onion, chopped

2 carrots, grated

500 g/1 lb 2 oz fresh beef mince

300 ml/10 fl oz hot beef stock

1 tbsp tomato purée

1 tbsp plain flour

salt and pepper

Crêpe batter
115 g/4 oz plain flour

pinch of salt

1 egg, lightly beaten

300 ml/10 fl oz milk

1 tsp sunflower oil

Upside-down Pie

1. Heat the oil in a saucepan. Add the onions and garlic and cook over a low heat, stirring occasionally, for 5 minutes, until softened. Add the beef, increase the heat to medium and cook, stirring frequently and breaking it up with a wooden spoon, for 8–10 minutes, until evenly browned.

2. Add the mushrooms and tomatoes and cook for a further 3 minutes, then stir in the anchovy essence, Worcestershire sauce, oregano, bay leaf, stock and wine. Season to taste with salt and pepper. Bring to the boil, then reduce the heat and simmer, stirring occasionally, for 20 minutes.

3. Meanwhile, preheat the oven to 180°C/350°F/Gas Mark 4. Sift the flour and salt into a bowl. Add the butter and rub it in with your fingertips until the mixture resembles breadcrumbs. Stir in the cheese, then add the egg yolk and enough of the milk to mix to a soft dough. Shape the dough into a 20-cm/8-inch round.

4. Transfer the beef mixture to a 20-cm/8-inch round cake tin and put the dough round on top. Bake in the preheated oven for 50 minutes, until the topping is golden brown. Remove the tin from the oven and invert onto a warmed serving dish. Cut into wedges and serve immediately.

Serves 4

3 tbsp sunflower oil
2 onions, finely chopped
1 garlic clove, finely chopped
350 g/12 oz fresh beef mince
55 g/2 oz mushrooms, finely chopped
4 tomatoes, peeled and diced
1 tsp anchovy essence
1 tbsp Worcestershire sauce
1 tsp dried oregano
1 bay leaf
150 ml/5 fl oz beef stock
150 ml/5 fl oz red wine
salt and pepper

Pastry
175 g/6 oz self-raising flour
pinch of salt
55 g/2 oz butter, cut into small pieces
85 g/3 oz Cheddar cheese, grated
1 egg yolk
100–150 ml/3½–5 fl oz milk

Beef & Cheese Cobbler

1. Preheat the oven to 180°C/350°F/Gas Mark 4. Heat the oil in a frying pan. Add the beef and cook over a medium heat, stirring frequently and breaking it up with a wooden spoon, for 8–10 minutes, until evenly browned.

2. Remove the pan from the heat and spoon the beef into a casserole, then stir in the plain flour. Add the onions, tomato ketchup, thyme and bay leaf and season to taste with salt and pepper. Pour in the stock and stir well, then cover and bake in the preheated oven for 1 hour.

3. Meanwhile, sift the self-raising flour, mustard powder and salt into a bowl. Add the butter and rub it in with your fingertips until the mixture resembles breadcrumbs. Stir in the cheese, Tabasco sauce and enough water to mix to a soft dough.

4. Roll out the dough to a thickness of 1 cm/½ inch on a lightly floured surface, then stamp out rounds with a 6-cm/2½-inch fluted round cutter.

5. Remove the casserole from the oven and take off the lid. Remove and discard the bay leaf. Cover the beef mixture with the dough rounds and brush them with milk. Return the casserole, without the lid, to the oven and bake for a further 35 minutes, until the topping is golden brown. Serve immediately.

Serves 4

2 tbsp sunflower oil

✳ 500 g/1 lb 2 oz fresh beef mince

2 tbsp plain flour

✳ 500 g/1 lb 2 oz onions, cut into wedges

2 tbsp tomato ketchup

1 tbsp chopped fresh thyme

1 bay leaf

300 ml/10 fl oz beef stock

✳ salt and pepper

Cobbler topping

225 g/8 oz self-raising flour, plus extra for dusting

½ tsp mustard powder

pinch of salt

40 g/1½ oz butter, cut into small pieces

85 g/3 oz Cheddar cheese, grated

dash of Tabasco sauce

milk, for glazing

53

French Meat Tart

1. Melt the butter with the oil in a large frying pan. Add the onions and garlic and cook over a low heat, stirring occasionally, for 5 minutes, until softened. Add the beef, increase the heat to medium and cook, stirring frequently and breaking it up with a wooden spoon, for 5 minutes. Add the sausage meat and cook, stirring frequently, for a further 3–5 minutes, until all the meat is evenly browned.

2. Mix the tomato purée with the water in a small bowl, then add to the pan with the sage. Season to taste with salt and pepper, reduce the heat and simmer for 10 minutes. Remove from the heat and leave to cool.

3. Meanwhile, roll out three quarters of the pastry on a lightly floured surface into a 5 mm/¼ inch thick round. Lift the dough into a 23-cm/9-inch loose-based fluted tart tin, easing it into the base and sides. Run the rolling pin over the rim to trim the edges. Chill in the refrigerator for 30 minutes.

4. Preheat the oven to 180°C/350°F/Gas Mark 4. Using a slotted spoon, transfer the beef mixture into the tart case, spreading it evenly. Roll out the remaining dough and cut it into 5 mm/¼ inch wide strips. Arrange the strips over the filling in a lattice, then brush with the egg white. Place on a baking sheet and bake in the preheated oven for 40 minutes, until golden. Serve immediately.

Serves 4

25 g/1 oz butter

2 tbsp olive oil

2 onions, chopped

1 garlic clove, finely chopped

300 g/10½ oz fresh beef mince

300 g/10½ oz sausage meat

1 tbsp tomato purée

2 tbsp water

1 tsp chopped fresh sage

350 g/12 oz ready-made shortcrust pastry, thawed if frozen

plain flour, for dusting

1 egg white, lightly beaten

salt and pepper

Greek Baked Pasta

1. Heat half the oil in a saucepan. Add the onion and garlic and cook over a low heat, stirring occasionally, for 5 minutes, until softened. Add the beef, increase the heat to medium and cook, stirring frequently and breaking it up with a wooden spoon, for 8–10 minutes, until evenly browned. Stir in the passata, sugar, vinegar and parsley and season to taste with salt and pepper. Reduce the heat, cover and simmer for 15 minutes, until thickened.

2. Meanwhile, preheat the oven to 180°C/350°F/Gas Mark 4. Preheat the grill. Brush a large ovenproof dish with oil. Bring a large pan of salted water to the boil. Add the macaroni, return to the boil and cook for 8–10 minutes, until tender but still firm to the bite. Drain and return to the pan. Stir in the remaining oil and the Gruyère.

3. Spread out the aubergine slices on a baking sheet and brush on both sides with oil. Cook under the preheated grill for 5 minutes on each side, until golden. Line the base and sides of the prepared dish with the aubergine slices.

4. Stir the eggs and Parmesan into the Béchamel sauce, then stir 3 tablespoons of the mixture into the beef mixture. Spoon half the macaroni evenly over the aubergine slices and pour in half the Béchamel mixture. Add the beef mixture and top with the remaining macaroni. Pour the remaining Béchamel mixture over the top. Bake in the preheated oven for 35–40 minutes, until golden brown. Leave to stand for 10 minutes before serving.

Serves 6

4 tbsp olive oil, plus extra for brushing

1 small onion, finely chopped

2 garlic cloves, finely chopped

500 g/1 lb 2 oz fresh beef mince

450 ml/16 fl oz passata

1 tsp sugar

2 tsp red wine vinegar

3 tbsp chopped fresh flat-leaf parsley

225 g/8 oz dried macaroni

225 g/8 oz Gruyère cheese, grated

1 kg/2 lb 4 oz aubergines, sliced lengthways

2 eggs, lightly beaten

100 g/3½ oz Parmesan cheese, grated

1 quantity Béchamel Sauce (see page 70)

salt and pepper

Bolognese Soufflé

1. Heat half the oil in a frying pan. Add the bacon and cook over a low heat, stirring occasionally, for 2–3 minutes. Add the onion and garlic and cook, stirring occasionally, for 5 minutes, until softened. Add the beef, increase the heat to medium and cook, stirring frequently and breaking it up with a wooden spoon, for 5–8 minutes, until evenly browned.

2. Stir in the tomatoes, tomato purée and thyme and season to taste with salt and pepper. Reduce the heat and simmer for 25 minutes, then remove from the heat and leave to cool.

3. Meanwhile, bring a saucepan of salted water to the boil. Add the pasta, return to the boil and cook for 8–10 minutes, until tender but still firm to the bite. Drain, return to the pan and toss with the remaining oil. Preheat the oven to 190°C/375°F/Gas Mark 5. Brush a soufflé dish with oil and sprinkle with the Parmesan.

4. Beat the egg yolks into the cooled beef mixture and fold in the pasta. Whisk the egg whites in a grease-free bowl until stiff, then fold into the beef and pasta mixture. Gently spoon into the prepared dish and bake in the preheated oven for 45 minutes, until risen and golden brown. Serve immediately.

Serves 4

2 tbsp olive oil, plus extra for brushing

4 bacon rashers, finely chopped

* 1 large onion, finely chopped

* 1 garlic clove, finely chopped

* 300 g/10½ oz fresh beef mince

400 g/14 oz canned chopped tomatoes

1 tbsp tomato purée

1 tbsp chopped fresh thyme

175 g/6 oz dried penne or other pasta shapes

25 g/1 oz Parmesan cheese, grated

3 eggs, separated

* salt and pepper

56

Beef & Beetroot Burgers

1. Heat 1 tablespoon of the oil in a frying pan. Add the onion and cook over a low heat, stirring occasionally, for 5 minutes, until softened.

2. Transfer the onion to a large bowl and add the beef, egg, vinegar, paprika and capers and mix well with your hands. Add the beetroot and soured cream, season to taste with salt and pepper and mix well again. Shape the mixture into four patties.

3. Melt 25 g/1 oz of the butter with the remaining oil in a frying pan. Add the burgers and cook over a medium heat for 6–7 minutes on each side, until well browned. Remove with a fish slice and drain on kitchen paper.

4. Melt half the remaining butter in a frying pan. Break two of the eggs into separate cups and slide them into the pan. Immediately collect the whites around the yolks with a slotted spoon to keep them neat and separated and cook for a few minutes until the whites have set but the yolks are still runny. Cook the remaining eggs in the remaining butter in the same way. Transfer the burgers to a warmed serving dish, top with the fried eggs and serve immediately.

Serves 4

3 tbsp sunflower oil

1 onion, finely chopped

650 g/1 lb 7 oz fresh beef mince

1 small egg, lightly beaten

2 tsp white wine vinegar

½ tsp paprika

1 tbsp finely chopped drained capers

3 tbsp finely chopped cooked beetroot

2 tbsp soured cream

55 g/2 oz butter

4 eggs

salt and pepper

Beef & Cheese Roll

1. Tear the bread into pieces, put it into a large bowl with the milk and leave to soak for 5 minutes. Squeeze out the excess milk from the bread and pour it off, reserving the soaked bread.

2. Meanwhile, lightly dust a sheet of greaseproof paper with flour. Add the beef, onion, mustard powder, parsley and eggs to the bowl with the bread. Season to taste with salt and pepper and mix well until thoroughly combined. Transfer the mixture to the greaseproof paper, shaping it into a neat rectangle, measuring about 20 x 25 cm/8 x 10 inches. Cover with another sheet of greaseproof paper and chill in the refrigerator for 1 hour.

3. Preheat the oven to 180°C/350°F/Gas Mark 4. Remove the meat mixture from the refrigerator and discard the top sheet of greaseproof paper. Cover the surface with mozzarella slices, then roll up, starting at a narrow edge and using the paper to help.

4. Carefully transfer the roll, seam-side down, to a shallow ovenproof dish or baking tin and brush with the melted butter. Bake in the preheated oven for 45–50 minutes, until golden brown and cooked through. Serve immediately with the tomato sauce.

Serves 4

100 g/3½ oz white bread (about 3½ thick slices), crusts removed

4 tbsp milk

plain flour, for dusting

* 650 g/1 lb 7 oz fresh beef mince

* 1 onion, finely chopped

2 tsp mustard powder

2 tbsp finely chopped fresh parsley

2 eggs, lightly beaten

225 g/8 oz mozzarella cheese, thinly sliced

25 g/1 oz butter, melted

* salt and pepper

1 quantity Tomato Sauce, to serve (see page 58)

Meal-in-a-bowl Beef & Herb Soup

1. Grate one of the onions into a bowl and finely chop the other. Heat the oil in a large saucepan. Add the chopped onion and cook over a low–medium heat, stirring occasionally, for 8–10 minutes, until golden. Stir in the turmeric and cumin, add the split peas and pour in the stock. Bring to the boil, then reduce the heat, cover and simmer for 15 minutes.

2. Meanwhile, add the beef to the grated onion, season to taste with salt and pepper and mix well. Shape the mixture into small balls.

3. Add the meatballs to the soup, re-cover the pan and simmer for a further 10 minutes. Add the rice and stir in the coriander, chives and spinach. Simmer, stirring frequently, for 25–30 minutes, until the rice is tender.

4. Melt the butter in a frying pan. Add the garlic and cook over a low heat, stirring frequently, for 2–3 minutes. Stir in the mint and cook for a further minute.

5. Transfer the soup to warmed bowls and sprinkle over the garlic mixture. Serve immediately with Greek-style yogurt.

Serves 6

* 2 onions
2 tbsp sunflower oil
1 tbsp ground turmeric
1 tsp ground cumin
100 g/3½ oz green or yellow split peas
1.2 litres/2 pints beef stock
* 225 g/8 oz fresh beef mince
200 g/7 oz long-grain rice
1 tbsp chopped fresh coriander
1 tbsp snipped fresh chives
55 g/2 oz baby spinach, finely chopped
25 g/1 oz butter
* 2 garlic cloves, finely chopped
3 tbsp chopped fresh mint
* salt and pepper
Greek-style yogurt, to serve

59

Dutch Crêpe Cake

1 First, make the crêpe batter. Sift the flour and salt into a bowl, then add the egg, egg yolk and 1 tablespoon of the milk and stir, gradually incorporating the dry ingredients and adding half the remaining milk. When the mixture is thick and smooth, beat in the remaining milk with a whisk. Set aside.

2 Meanwhile, melt the butter a frying pan. Add the onions and cook over a low–medium heat, stirring occasionally, for 8–10 minutes, until golden. Add the beef and cook, stirring frequently and breaking it up with a wooden spoon, for 8–10 minutes, until evenly browned. Add the mushrooms and cook for a further 5 minutes, then drain off as much fat as possible. Stir in the parsley and cream and season to taste with salt and pepper. Reduce the heat, cover and simmer, stirring occasionally, for 20 minutes.

3 Heat a large frying pan, then add half the melted butter. Stir the batter and pour half into the hot pan, then tilt and rotate the pan to cover the base evenly. Cook for 2 minutes, until the underside is golden brown, then flip over the crêpe and cook on the other side for 2 minutes. Slide onto a warmed plate.

4 Add the remaining melted butter to the pan and pour in the remaining batter. Cook for 3 minutes, then flip over and spoon the meat mixture evenly on top of the crêpe. Top with the first crêpe and carefully slide onto a warmed plate. Garnish with parsley, cut into wedges and serve immediately.

Serves 4

25 g/1 oz butter
* 2 onions, finely chopped
* 650 g/1 lb 7 oz fresh beef mince
85 g/3 oz mushrooms, thinly sliced
2 tbsp chopped fresh parsley, plus extra to garnish
150 ml/5 fl oz double cream
1 tbsp melted butter
* salt and pepper

Crêpe batter
115 g/4 oz plain flour
pinch of salt
1 egg
1 egg yolk
125 ml/4 fl oz milk

Beef & Vegetable Gratin

1. Heat the oil in a large saucepan. Add the garlic and onions and cook over a low heat, stirring occasionally, for 8–10 minutes, until golden brown. Add the beef, increase the heat to medium and cook, stirring frequently and breaking it up with a wooden spoon, for 8–10 minutes, until evenly browned. Stir in the courgettes, carrots, red pepper and raisins and season to taste with salt and pepper. Reduce the heat, cover and simmer for 25 minutes.

2. Meanwhile, preheat the oven to 180°C/350°F/Gas Mark 4. Melt the butter in a saucepan. Add the flour and cook over a low heat, stirring constantly, for 2 minutes. Remove the pan from the heat and gradually stir in the milk, a little at a time, until smooth. Return the pan to the heat and bring to the boil, stirring constantly, then cook, stirring, for a few minutes more, until thickened. Remove the pan from the heat and stir in the cheese until melted.

3. Stir the sweetcorn, beans and parsley into the beef mixture and simmer for a further 3 minutes, then remove the pan from the heat. Spoon the mixture into an ovenproof dish.

4. Lightly beat the egg yolks in a bowl with a fork, then stir in 4 tablespoons of the cheese sauce. Stir the egg yolk mixture into the cheese sauce and pour it over the meat mixture to cover. Bake in the preheated oven for 25–30 minutes, until the topping is golden brown. Serve immediately.

Serves 6–8

3 tbsp sunflower oil

2 garlic cloves, finely chopped

2 onions, sliced

1 kg/2 lb 4 oz fresh beef mince

500 g/1 lb 2 oz courgettes, thinly sliced

300 g/10½ oz carrots, thinly sliced

1 red pepper, deseeded and thinly sliced

55 g/2 oz raisins

85 g/3 oz butter

85 g/3 oz plain flour

850 ml/1½ pints milk

115 g/4 oz Cheddar cheese, grated

350 g/12 oz canned sweetcorn, drained

400 g/14 oz canned cannellini beans, drained and rinsed

2 tbsp chopped fresh parsley

4 egg yolks

salt and pepper

61

Beef & Spinach Cannelloni

① Cook the spinach in just the water clinging to the leaves for 5–8 minutes, until tender, then drain and squeeze out as much liquid as possible. Chop finely.

② Melt 15 g/½ oz of the butter with the oil in a large frying pan. Add the shallots and garlic and cook over a low heat, stirring occasionally, for 5 minutes, until softened. Add the beef, increase the heat to medium and cook, stirring frequently and breaking it up with a wooden spoon, for 8–10 minutes, until evenly browned. Add the spinach and cook for 3–4 minutes. Transfer the mixture to a bowl and stir in 3 tablespoons of the Parmesan, 1½ tablespoons of the cream, the egg and oregano. Season to taste with salt and pepper.

③ Preheat the oven to 190°C/375°F/Gas Mark 5. Melt 25 g/ 1 oz of the remaining butter in a saucepan, then stir in the flour and cook, stirring constantly, for 2 minutes. Remove the pan from the heat and gradually stir in the milk and the remaining cream, until smooth. Return the pan to the heat and bring to the boil, stirring constantly. Remove from the heat.

④ Fill the cannelloni tubes with the beef mixture. Pour a little of the tomato sauce over the base of an ovenproof dish, then put the cannelloni in the dish in two layers. Spoon the white sauce over them and top with the remaining tomato sauce. Sprinkle with the remaining Parmesan and dot with the remaining butter. Bake in the preheated oven for 30 minutes. Serve immediately.

Serves 4

175 g/6 oz spinach, coarse stalks removed

55 g/2 oz butter

1½ tbsp olive oil

✳ 2 shallots, finely chopped

✳ 2 garlic cloves, finely chopped

✳ 225 g/8 oz fresh beef mince

115 g/4 oz Parmesan cheese, finely grated

4½ tbsp double cream

1 egg, lightly beaten

pinch of dried oregano

4 tbsp plain flour

175 ml/6 fl oz milk

16 no pre-cook cannelloni tubes

1 quantity Tomato Sauce (see page 58)

✳ salt and pepper

Spicy

62

Taco Soup

1. Heat the oil in a large saucepan. Add the onion and cook over a low heat, stirring occasionally, for 5 minutes, until softened. Add the beef, increase the heat to medium and cook, stirring frequently and breaking it up with a wooden spoon, for 8–10 minutes. Drain off as much fat as possible.

2. Stir in the tomatoes, kidney beans with their can juices, tomato juice, sugar, spices and stock and bring to the boil. Reduce the heat, cover and simmer, stirring occasionally, for 15 minutes.

3. Meanwhile, put the cheese, tortilla chips and soured cream into separate serving dishes. Peel, stone and dice the avocado and gently toss with the lemon juice in a bowl.

4. Remove the soup from the heat and ladle into warmed soup bowls. Scatter the avocado over the soup and serve immediately with the cheese, tortilla chips and soured cream.

Serves 4–6

1 tbsp sunflower oil

1 small onion, finely chopped

225 g/8 oz fresh beef mince

400 g/14 oz canned chopped tomatoes

400 g/14 oz canned red kidney beans

225 ml/8 fl oz tomato juice

1 tsp sugar

¼ tsp ground cinnamon

¼ tsp ground cumin

1 tsp chilli powder

350 ml/12 fl oz beef stock

115 g/4 oz Cheddar cheese, coarsely grated

350 g/12 oz tortilla chips

225 ml/8 fl oz soured cream

1 avocado

2 tbsp lemon juice

63

Chilli Burgers

1. Preheat the grill. Mix together the onion, breadcrumbs, coriander, chilli powder, garlic salt, cumin and milk in a bowl. Add the beef and mix well with your hands until thoroughly combined.

2. Divide the mixture into four portions and shape into patties. Cook under the preheated grill for 5–8 minutes on each side, until cooked to your liking.

3. Spread the base of each bun with a little guacamole and top with the lettuce leaves, burgers and tomato slices. Cover with the tops of the buns. Serve immediately with tortilla chips.

Serves 4

* 1 small onion, finely chopped
55 g/2 oz fresh breadcrumbs
2 tbsp chopped fresh coriander
½ tsp chilli powder or cayenne pepper
½ tsp garlic salt
1 tsp ground cumin
100 ml/3½ fl oz milk
* 1 kg/2 lb 4 oz fresh beef mince

To serve
4 hamburger buns, split and toasted
guacamole
lettuce leaves
tomato slices
tortilla chips

Enchiladas

1. Heat 1 tablespoon of the oil in a frying pan. Add three quarters of the onions and half the garlic and cook over a low heat, stirring occasionally, for 5 minutes. Add the beef, increase the heat to medium and cook, stirring frequently and breaking it up with a wooden spoon, for 8–10 minutes, until evenly browned. Remove the pan from the heat and transfer the mixture to a bowl. Stir in the Cheddar cheese and three quarters of the chillies and season to taste with salt and pepper.

2. Heat the remaining oil in a saucepan. Add the remaining onion, garlic and chilli and cook over a medium heat, stirring occasionally, for 7–8 minutes. Stir in the tomatoes, tomato purée, oregano, Tabasco sauce and sugar, then season to taste with salt and cook for a further 3 minutes. Stir in the cream, then reduce the heat, cover and simmer, stirring occasionally, for 15 minutes. Remove from the heat and leave to cool slightly.

3. Meanwhile, preheat the oven to 180°C/350°F/Gas Mark 4. Heat a frying pan and brush with oil. One at a time, dip the tortillas in the tomato sauce, shake off any excess and cook for 30 seconds on each side. Transfer to a large plate, put a tablespoon of the beef mixture in the centre and roll up. Put the filled tortillas in a large ovenproof dish and pour the remaining tomato sauce over them. Sprinkle with the Parmesan and bake in the preheated oven for 15–20 minutes. Serve immediately.

Serves 6

- 4 tbsp corn oil, plus extra for brushing
- 2 onions, finely chopped
- 2 garlic cloves, finely chopped
- 225 g/8 oz fresh beef mince
- 55 g/2 oz Cheddar cheese, grated
- 4 fresh red chillies, deseeded and finely chopped
- 400 g/14 oz canned chopped tomatoes
- 115 g/4 oz tomato purée
- pinch of dried oregano
- dash of Tabasco sauce
- 1 tsp sugar
- 125 ml/4 fl oz double cream
- 18 flour tortillas or corn tortillas
- 2 tbsp grated Parmesan cheese
- salt and pepper

Chilli con Carne

1. Heat the oil in a large saucepan. Add the onions and garlic and cook over a low heat, stirring occasionally, for 5 minutes, until softened. Add the beef, increase the heat to medium and cook, stirring frequently and breaking it up with a wooden spoon, for 8–10 minutes, until evenly browned.

2. Stir in the tomatoes, tomato purée, cumin, cayenne pepper, chilli powder, oregano, bay leaf and stock, then season to taste with salt and bring to the boil. Reduce the heat, cover and simmer, stirring occasionally, for 1 hour.

3. Add the kidney beans, re-cover the pan and simmer, stirring occasionally, for a further 30 minutes. Remove and discard the bay leaf and serve immediately with rice.

Serves 6

2 tbsp corn oil

✳ 2 onions, thinly sliced

✳ 2 garlic cloves, finely chopped

✳ 650 g/1 lb 7 oz fresh beef mince

200 g/7 oz canned chopped tomatoes

5 tbsp tomato purée

1 tsp ground cumin

1 tsp cayenne pepper

1 tbsp chilli powder

1 tsp dried oregano

1 bay leaf

350 ml/12 fl oz beef stock

400 g/14 oz canned red kidney beans, drained and rinsed

✳ salt

cooked rice, to serve

66

Fiery Beef Tacos

1. Heat the oil in a frying pan. Add the onion and garlic and cook over a low heat, stirring occasionally, for 5 minutes, until softened. Add the beef, increase the heat to medium and cook, stirring frequently and breaking it up with a wooden spoon, for 8–10 minutes, until evenly browned. Drain off as much fat as possible.

2. Stir in the chilli powder and cumin, season to taste with salt and pepper and cook over a low heat, stirring frequently for a further 8 minutes, then remove from the heat.

3. Heat the taco shells according to the packet instructions. Meanwhile, peel, stone and slice the avocado and gently toss with the lemon juice in a bowl.

4. Divide the lettuce, spring onions, tomatoes and avocado slices among the taco shells. Add a tablespoon of soured cream to each, then divide the beef mixture among them. Sprinkle with the cheese and serve immediately.

Serves 4

2 tbsp corn oil

* 1 small onion, finely chopped
* 2 garlic cloves, finely chopped
* 280 g/10 oz fresh beef mince

1½ tsp hot chilli powder

1 tsp ground cumin

8 taco shells

1 avocado

2 tbsp lemon juice

¼ head of lettuce, shredded

4 spring onions, thinly sliced

2 tomatoes, peeled and diced

125 ml/4 fl oz soured cream

115 g/4 oz Cheddar cheese, grated

* salt and pepper

Burritos

1. Soak the beans overnight in a bowl of cold water, then drain. Put the beans into a large saucepan and pour in water to cover. Bring to the boil and boil vigorously for 15 minutes, then drain and return to the pan. Add fresh water to cover and bring to the boil. Reduce the heat, cover and simmer for 1–1½ hours, until tender, then drain.

2. Heat the oil in a large saucepan. Add the onion, garlic and red pepper and cook over a low heat, stirring occasionally, for 5 minutes, until softened. Add the beef, increase the heat to medium and cook, stirring frequently and breaking it up with a wooden spoon, for 8–10 minutes, until evenly browned. Reduce the heat, stir in the spices, oregano and tomato ketchup and season to taste with salt. Add the wine, tomatoes, bay leaf and beans and mix well. Cover and simmer, stirring occasionally, for 25 minutes. Stir in the jalapeño chillies and coriander and remove from the heat. Remove and discard the bay leaf.

3. Meanwhile, preheat the oven to 180°C/350°F/Gas Mark 4. Brush a large ovenproof dish with oil. Using a slotted spoon, divide the meat mixture among the tortillas and roll up. Put them in the prepared dish, seam-side down, and sprinkle with the cheese. Bake in the preheated oven for 15 minutes. Serve immediately with the guacamole and salsa.

Serves 6

225 g/8 oz dried black beans

2 tbsp vegetable oil, plus extra for brushing

* 1 Spanish onion, chopped

* 2 garlic cloves, finely chopped

1 red pepper, deseeded and chopped

* 550 g/1 lb 4 oz fresh beef mince

1 tbsp ground cumin

1 tsp paprika

¼ tsp cayenne pepper

pinch of dried oregano

2 tbsp tomato ketchup

100 ml/3½ fl oz red wine

400 g/14 oz canned chopped tomatoes

1 bay leaf

3 tbsp chopped pickled jalapeño chillies

1 tbsp chopped fresh coriander

12 flour tortillas

70 g/2½ oz Cheddar cheese, grated

* salt

guacamole and salsa, to serve

Empanadas

1. Heat the oil in a large frying pan. Add the onion, garlic and red pepper and cook over a low heat, stirring occasionally, for 5 minutes. Add the beef, increase the heat to medium and cook, stirring frequently and breaking it up with a wooden spoon, for 8–10 minutes, until evenly browned. Drain off as much fat as possible.

2. Stir the tomatoes, raisins, chilli powder and cumin into the pan, then season to taste with salt and pepper, reduce the heat and simmer for 10 minutes. Remove the pan from the heat.

3. Meanwhile, preheat the oven to 190°C/375°F/Gas Mark 5. Brush a large baking sheet with oil. Roll out the pastry on a lightly floured surface and stamp out eight rounds with a 13-cm/5-inch plain cutter. Put a tablespoon of the beef mixture on one side of each dough round, brush the edges with water and fold over. Press the edges with a fork or your finger to seal.

4. Transfer to the prepared baking sheet and bake in the preheated oven for 30–35 minutes, until golden brown. Serve immediately.

Makes 8

2 tbsp corn oil, plus extra for brushing

* 1 onion, finely chopped

* 1 garlic clove, finely chopped

½ small red pepper, deseeded and diced

* 225 g/8 oz fresh beef mince

2 tomatoes, peeled and diced

55 g/2 oz raisins

½–1 tsp chilli powder

pinch of ground cumin

300 g/10½ oz ready-made puff pastry, thawed if frozen

plain flour, for dusting

* salt and pepper

Nachos

1. Preheat the oven to 180°C/350°F/Gas Mark 4. Heat the oil in a large frying pan. Add the onion and garlic, if using, and cook over a low heat, stirring occasionally, for 5 minutes, until softened. Add the beef, increase the heat to medium and cook, stirring frequently and breaking it up with a wooden spoon, for 8–10 minutes, until evenly browned. Remove from the heat, drain off as much fat as possible and season to taste with salt and pepper.

2. Spread out the tortilla chips in a large ovenproof dish and spoon the refried beans evenly over them. Sprinkle with half the cheese, cover with the beef mixture and sprinkle with the remaining cheese. Sprinkle with the jalapeño chillies and bake in the preheated oven for 10–15 minutes, until the cheese has melted. Serve immediately with soured cream, guacamole and salsa.

Serves 4–6

1 tbsp corn oil

✳ 1 onion, finely chopped

✳ 1 garlic clove, finely chopped (optional)

✳ 500 g/1 lb 2 oz fresh beef mince

450 g/1 lb tortilla chips

400 g/14 oz canned refried beans

225 g/8 oz Cheddar cheese, coarsely grated

4 tbsp chopped pickled jalapeño chillies

✳ salt and pepper

soured cream, guacamole and salsa, to serve

Mexican Beef Stew

1　Heat the oil in a large saucepan. Add the onion, garlic and green pepper and cook over a low heat, stirring occasionally, for 5 minutes. Add the beef, increase the heat to medium and cook, stirring frequently and breaking it up with a wooden spoon, for 8–10 minutes, until evenly browned.

2　Stir in the chillies, cumin seeds, coriander, sweetcorn, kidney beans, tomato purée and stock, then season to taste with salt and pepper. Reduce the heat, cover and simmer, stirring occasionally, for 50–60 minutes. Serve immediately.

Serves 4

2 tbsp corn oil

* 1 onion, finely chopped

* 2 garlic cloves, finely chopped

1 green pepper, deseeded and finely chopped

* 500 g/1 lb 2 oz fresh beef mince

3 fresh green chillies, deseeded and finely chopped

1 tsp cumin seeds, lightly toasted

1 tbsp chopped fresh coriander

140 g/5 oz canned sweetcorn, drained

200 g/7 oz canned red kidney beans, drained and rinsed

1 tbsp tomato purée

450 ml/16 fl oz beef stock

* salt and pepper

Beef Tamale

① Heat the oil in a large frying pan. Add the onion and cook over a low heat, stirring occasionally, for 5 minutes, until softened. Add the beef, increase the heat to medium and cook, stirring frequently and breaking it up with a wooden spoon, for 8–10 minutes, until evenly browned.

② Stir in the ham, capers, sultanas, olives, tomato purée, chilli powder, thyme and sugar and season to taste with salt and pepper. Reduce the heat and simmer, stirring frequently, for 5 minutes. Stir in the sweetcorn, then remove the pan from the heat and stir in the eggs.

③ Cut out four 15-cm/6-inch squares of double-layer greaseproof paper. Divide the mixture among them and gather together the edges and tie with kitchen string. Put them into a steamer set over a pan of boiling water, cover and steam for 45–50 minutes. Remove from the steamer and serve immediately.

Serves 4

2 tbsp corn oil

✳ 1 large onion, finely chopped

✳ 450 g/1 lb fresh beef mince

175 g/6 oz ham, finely diced

1 tbsp drained capers

4 tbsp sultanas

1 tbsp chopped stoned green olives

4 tbsp tomato purée

¼–½ tsp chilli powder

2 tsp chopped fresh thyme

1 tsp sugar

325 g/11½ oz canned sweetcorn, drained

3 eggs, lightly beaten

✳ salt and pepper

72

Spicy Beef & Sweet Potatoes

1. Preheat the oven to 200°C/400°F/Gas Mark 6. Prick the sweet potatoes all over with a fork. Put them directly on an oven shelf and bake in the preheated oven for 1 hour, until soft.

2. Meanwhile, put the tomatoes, chillies, peppercorns, allspice berries, cinnamon stick and ground coriander into a saucepan and bring to the boil. Reduce the heat and simmer, stirring occasionally, for 30 minutes, until thickened. Remove the pan from the heat and discard the cinnamon stick, then press the sauce through a nylon sieve into a bowl.

3. Heat half the oil in a frying pan. Add the beef and cook over a medium heat, stirring frequently and breaking it up with a wooden spoon, for 8–10 minutes, until evenly browned. Stir in the tomato mixture and tomato purée and season to taste with salt. Simmer, stirring frequently, for 20 minutes.

4. Remove the sweet potatoes from the oven. When they are cool enough to handle, peel off the skins and chop the flesh.

5. Heat the remaining oil in a frying pan. Add the onion and garlic and cook over a low heat, stirring occasionally, for 5 minutes, until softened. Add the sweet potatoes and stock and cook, stirring constantly, for 5 minutes. Season to taste with salt, remove from the heat and transfer the mixture to a warmed serving dish. Top with the beef mixture and serve immediately with soured cream.

Serves 4

4 sweet potatoes

800 g/1 lb 12 oz canned chopped tomatoes

2 fresh green chillies, deseeded and chopped

6 black peppercorns

6 allspice berries

1 cinnamon stick

1 tsp ground coriander

2 tbsp sunflower oil

✳ 650 g/1 lb 7 oz fresh beef mince

1 tbsp tomato purée

✳ 1 onion, finely chopped

✳ 1 garlic clove, finely chopped

4 tbsp beef stock

✳ salt

soured cream, to serve

Bobotie

1. Preheat the oven to 180°C/350°F/Gas Mark 4. Grease a 2.5-litre/4½-pint pie dish with butter. Tear the bread into pieces, put it into a bowl with the milk and leave to soak.

2. Melt the butter with the oil in a frying pan. Add the onions and garlic and cook over a medium heat, stirring occasionally, for 8–10 minutes, until lightly browned. Remove from the heat and transfer the onions and garlic to a bowl. Add the curry powder, beef, sultanas, almonds, parsley, lemon juice, vinegar and sugar to the bowl, then season to taste with salt and pepper. Mix well until thoroughly combined, then squeeze out the bread, reserving the milk, and stir it into the mixture. Lightly beat one of the eggs and stir it into the mixture, then transfer to the prepared dish, pressing it down well.

3. Measure the remaining milk and make it up to 175 ml/6 fl oz with extra milk if necessary, then beat in the remaining egg. Pour the mixture over the meat.

4. Stand the dish in a roasting tin and pour in boiling water to come about halfway up the side. Bake in the preheated oven for 1 hour, until the topping is golden brown. Serve immediately.

Serves 4–6

85 g/3 oz white bread (about 3 thick slices), crusts removed

300 ml/10 fl oz milk, plus extra if needed

55 g/2 oz butter, plus extra for greasing

1 tbsp sunflower oil

2 onions, chopped

1 garlic clove, finely chopped

1½ tbsp curry powder

1 kg/2 lb 4 oz fresh beef mince

115 g/4 oz sultanas

55 g/2 oz slivered almonds

1 tbsp chopped fresh parsley

2 tbsp lemon juice

1 tbsp white wine vinegar

1 tbsp sugar

2 eggs

salt and pepper

Indonesian Beef Parcels

1. Put the shallots, garlic, beef, cumin, ground coriander and curry powder into a bowl, then season to taste with salt and pepper and mix well until combined. Heat a wok over a medium heat, then add the beef mixture and cook, stirring constantly, for 8–10 minutes, until the meat is evenly browned. Remove from the heat and leave to cool, then stir in just enough of the beaten egg to bind, reserving the remainder.

2. Preheat the oven to 200°C/400°F/Gas Mark 6. Lightly dust a baking sheet with flour. Brush one sheet of filo with oil, put a second sheet on top and cut the double layer in half. Put a spoonful of the beef mixture in the centre of each piece and fold the sides into the middle. Brush the edges with beaten egg and fold the top and bottom into the middle. Put the parcels on the prepared baking sheet and place in the refrigerator while you make more parcels in the same way.

3. Brush the tops of the parcels with beaten egg and bake in the preheated oven for 20 minutes, until golden brown. Transfer to a warmed serving dish and serve immediately.

Makes 16

* 4 shallots, finely chopped
* 2 garlic cloves, finely chopped
* 500 g/1 lb 2 oz fresh beef mince
  1 tsp ground cumin
  1 tsp ground coriander
  2 tsp curry powder
  2–3 eggs, lightly beaten
  plain flour, for dusting
  16 sheets filo pastry
  groundnut oil, for brushing
* salt and pepper

75

Curry Puffs

1. Heat the oil in a frying pan. Add the onion, garlic, ginger and chillies and cook over a low heat, stirring occasionally, for 5 minutes, until softened. Stir in the chilli powder, ground coriander and turmeric, season to taste with salt and cook, stirring occasionally, for a further 3 minutes.

2. Add the beef, increase the heat to medium and cook, stirring frequently and breaking it up with a wooden spoon, for 8–10 minutes, until evenly browned. Stir in the tomato, peas and lime juice, reduce the heat and cook, stirring occasionally, for a further 5 minutes. Remove the pan from the heat.

3. Preheat the oven to 200°C/400°F/Gas Mark 6. Roll out the pastry on a lightly floured surface to a thickness of about 3 mm/⅛ inch. Stamp out 20 rounds with a 10-cm/4-inch pastry cutter.

4. Put 2 teaspoons of the beef mixture slightly to the side of each round. Brush the edges with water and fold over, pressing the edges to seal. Crimp the edges with a fork. Put the puffs on a baking sheet, brush with the beaten egg and bake in the preheated oven for 20–30 minutes, until golden brown. Remove from the oven, transfer to a wire rack and leave to cool slightly. Serve warm.

Makes 20

2 tbsp groundnut oil

* 1 onion, finely chopped

* 1 garlic clove, finely chopped

1-cm/½-inch piece fresh ginger, finely chopped

2 fresh red chillies, deseeded and finely chopped

1 tsp chilli powder

½ tsp ground coriander

½ tsp ground turmeric

* 225 g/8 oz fresh beef mince

1 tomato, peeled and diced

55 g/2 oz frozen peas, thawed

2 tbsp lime juice

500 g/1 lb 2 oz ready-made puff pastry, thawed if frozen

plain flour, for dusting

1 egg, lightly beaten

* salt

Indian Kebabs

1. Put the onion, garlic, ginger, chillies, turmeric, coriander, yogurt, lemon juice, beef and breadcrumbs into a bowl. Season to taste with salt and mix well with your hands until thoroughly combined. Cover with clingfilm and leave to rest at room temperature for 30 minutes.

2. Preheat the grill. Brush 12 metal or pre-soaked wooden skewers with melted butter. Dampen your hands and shape the beef mixture into 24 cigar shapes. Thread two onto each prepared skewer and place them in the grill pan

3. Brush with a little melted butter and cook under the preheated grill for 5 minutes. Turn the skewers, brush with more melted butter and cook for a further 4 minutes, until the kebabs are cooked through and browned.

4. Transfer the kebabs to a warmed serving dish, drizzle with yogurt and garnish with coriander. Serve immediately with tomato and onion salad and naan bread.

Serves 4

* 1 onion, finely chopped
* 2 garlic cloves, finely chopped
* 4-cm/1½-inch piece fresh ginger, finely chopped
* 2 fresh green chillies, deseeded and finely chopped
* ½ tsp ground turmeric
* 2 tbsp chopped fresh coriander, plus extra to garnish
* 3 tbsp natural yogurt, plus extra to serve
* 1 tbsp lemon juice
* 650 g/1 lb 7 oz fresh beef mince
* 4 tbsp fresh breadcrumbs
* melted butter, for brushing
* salt
* tomato and onion salad and warm naan bread, to serve

Beef Curry

1. Heat the oil in a frying pan. Add the onions, garlic and ginger and cook over a low heat, stirring occasionally, for 5 minutes, until softened. Add the ground coriander, chilli powder and turmeric and cook, stirring occasionally, for a further 3 minutes.

2. Add the beef, increase the heat to medium and cook, stirring frequently and breaking it up with a wooden spoon, for 8–10 minutes, until evenly browned. Stir in the tomatoes and season to taste with salt. Reduce the heat, cover and simmer, stirring occasionally, for 15 minutes. Uncover the pan and cook for a further 5 minutes.

3. Taste and adjust the seasoning, adding more salt if needed. Transfer the curry to a warmed serving dish, sprinkle with the chopped coriander and serve immediately with rice.

Serves 4

3 tbsp corn oil

4 onions, thinly sliced

2 garlic cloves, finely chopped

2.5-cm/1-inch piece fresh ginger, finely chopped

1 tsp ground coriander

1 tsp chilli powder

1 tsp ground turmeric

650 g/1 lb 7 oz fresh beef mince

200 g/7 oz canned chopped tomatoes

2 tbsp chopped fresh coriander

salt

cooked rice, to serve

78

Indian Potato Cakes

1. Cook the potatoes in a large saucepan of salted boiling water for 20–25 minutes, until tender but not falling apart. Drain, return to the pan and mash well.

2. Heat 1 tablespoon of the oil in a large frying pan. Add the onion, garlic, chillies, ginger, cumin, ground coriander, mint and chopped coriander and cook over a low heat, stirring occasionally, for 5 minutes. Add the beef, increase the heat to medium and cook, stirring frequently and breaking it up with a wooden spoon, for 5 minutes. Add the peas and cook, stirring frequently, for a further 3–5 minutes, until the meat is evenly browned and the mixture is dry. Remove from the heat, season to taste with salt and stir in the lemon juice.

3. Divide the mashed potato into 10 portions. Put one portion in your hand and flatten it into a round. Put a spoonful of the beef mixture in the middle and re-shape to enclose the filling completely. Make nine more potato cakes in the same way.

4. Lightly beat the eggs in a shallow dish. Spread out the breadcrumbs in a separate shallow dish. Dip the potato cakes first in the beaten egg and then in the breadcrumbs to coat. Chill in the refrigerator for 30 minutes.

5. Heat the remaining oil in a frying pan. Add the potato cakes, in batches, and cook over a medium heat, turning occasionally, until golden brown all over. Serve immediately.

Makes 10

1 kg/2 lb 4 oz potatoes, cut into chunks
100 ml/3½ fl oz groundnut oil
* 1 large onion, finely chopped
* 2 garlic cloves, finely chopped
2 fresh green chillies, deseeded and finely chopped
4-cm/1½-inch piece fresh ginger, finely chopped
1 tsp ground cumin
1 tsp ground coriander
2 tbsp chopped fresh mint
1 tbsp chopped fresh coriander
* 225 g/8 oz fresh beef mince
55 g/2 oz frozen peas, thawed
4 tbsp lemon juice
2 eggs
115 g/4 oz fresh breadcrumbs
* salt

Beef Samosas

1. For the dough, sift together the flour and salt into a bowl and make a well in the centre. Pour the oil into the well and add the water. Gradually incorporate the dry ingredients into the liquid, adding a little more water if necessary. Turn out onto a lightly floured surface and knead until smooth and elastic. Shape into a ball and leave to rest for 30 minutes.

2. Meanwhile, heat the oil in a large frying pan. Add the onion, garlic and ginger and cook over a low heat, stirring occasionally, for 5 minutes, until softened. Stir in the chilli powder, turmeric, ground coriander and garam masala and cook, stirring occasionally, for 3 minutes. Add the beef, increase the heat to medium and cook, stirring frequently and breaking it up with a wooden spoon, for 8–10 minutes, until evenly browned. Stir in the lemon juice and mint and leave to cool.

3. Divide the dough into 14 pieces. Roll out each piece into an oval about 20 cm/8 inches long, then cut in half widthways. Brush the straight edge of one piece with water and fold in each side to make a cone. Put a tablespoonful of the beef mixture into the cone, brush the open side with water and press to seal. Make 27 more samosas in the same way.

4. Heat enough oil for deep-frying in a deep-fat fryer to 180–190°C/350–375°F, or until a cube of bread browns in 30 seconds. Add the samosas, in batches, and cook until crisp and golden brown. Serve immediately with chilli sauce.

Makes 28

2 tbsp sunflower oil, plus extra for deep-frying

* 1 onion, chopped

* 2 garlic cloves, finely chopped

4-cm/1½-inch piece fresh ginger, grated

1 tsp chilli powder

1 tsp ground turmeric

1 tsp ground coriander

1 tsp garam masala

* 500 g/1 lb 2 oz fresh beef mince

juice of ½ lemon

3 tbsp chopped fresh mint

chilli sauce, to serve

Dough
225 g/8 oz plain flour, plus extra for dusting

large pinch of salt

2 tbsp sunflower oil

about 5 tbsp warm water

Spiced Beef & Pistachio Nuts

1 Preheat the oven to 190°C/375°F/Gas Mark 5. Melt the butter in a saucepan. Add the onion, garlic and chillies and cook over a low heat, stirring occasionally, for 5 minutes. Add the beef, increase the heat to medium and cook, stirring frequently and breaking it up with a wooden spoon, for 5–8 minutes, until evenly browned.

2 Remove the pan from the heat, stir in the pistachio nuts, garam masala, tomatoes, breadcrumbs and soured cream and season to taste with salt and pepper. Mix well until thoroughly combined, then spoon the mixture into an ovenproof dish. Bake in the preheated oven for 35–45 minutes, until the top is lightly browned. Serve immediately, garnished with pistachio nuts.

Serves 4

55 g/2 oz butter

✳ 1 Spanish onion, chopped

✳ 2 garlic cloves, chopped

3 fresh green chillies, deseeded and chopped

✳ 1 kg/2 lb 4 oz fresh beef mince

2 tbsp roughly chopped pistachio nuts, plus extra to garnish

1½ tbsp garam masala

4 tomatoes, peeled and diced

4 tbsp fresh breadcrumbs

4 tbsp soured cream

✳ salt and pepper

Pasta with Aromatic Beef Sauce

1. Heat the oil in a frying pan. Add the shallots and garlic and cook over a low heat, stirring occasionally, for 5 minutes, until softened. Add the beef, increase the heat to medium and cook, stirring frequently and breaking it up with a wooden spoon, for 8–10 minutes, until evenly browned. Drain off as much fat as possible.

2. Stir in the wine and simmer over a low heat, stirring frequently, for 5 minutes. Add the mushrooms, cinnamon, allspice, parsley, torn basil, tomatoes and tomato ketchup, then season to taste with salt and pepper and mix well. Cover and simmer over a very low heat, stirring occasionally, for 1 hour. If the mixture seems to be drying out, add a little water.

3. Meanwhile, bring a large saucepan of salted water to the boil. Add the pasta, return to the boil and cook for 8–10 minutes, until tender but still firm to the bite. Drain and toss with the beef sauce. Garnish with basil sprigs and serve immediately.

Serves 4

2 tbsp sunflower oil

4 shallots, finely chopped

1 garlic clove, finely chopped

450 g/1 lb fresh beef mince

3 tbsp red wine

115 g/4 oz mushrooms, chopped

½ tsp ground cinnamon

½ tsp ground allspice

1 tbsp chopped fresh parsley

1 fresh basil sprig, leaves torn, plus extra sprigs to garnish

400 g/14 oz canned chopped tomatoes

2 tbsp tomato ketchup

350 g/12 oz dried conchiglie or other pasta shapes

salt and pepper

82

Meatball Goulash

1. Tear the bread into pieces and put it into a small bowl. Add the milk and leave to soak for 5 minutes, then squeeze out the excess milk and put the bread into a large bowl. Add the beef, two thirds of the garlic, the egg, orange rind and 1 teaspoon of the dill. Season to taste with salt and pepper and mix well until thoroughly combined. Shape the mixture into small balls and put them on a plate. Cover with clingfilm and chill in the refrigerator for 30 minutes.

2. Heat the oil in a large flameproof casserole. Add the onions, the remaining garlic and the carrots and cook over a low heat, stirring occasionally, for 5 minutes, until softened. Stir in the mushrooms and paprika and cook, stirring occasionally, for a further 3 minutes. Pour in the stock and wine, add the caraway seeds and the remaining dill and bring to the boil over a medium heat, stirring constantly.

3. Add the meatballs to the casserole and bring back to the boil, then reduce the heat, cover and simmer for 1 hour. Add the potatoes, re-cover the pan and simmer for 20–25 minutes, until tender.

4. Mix the cornflour to a paste with the water in a small bowl and add to the casserole with the soured cream. Cook, stirring constantly, for 2–3 minutes, until thickened, but do not allow to boil. Garnish with paprika and parsley and serve immediately.

Serves 4

4 slices rye bread, crusts removed

3 tbsp milk

* 1 kg/2 lb 4 oz fresh beef mince

* 3 garlic cloves, finely chopped

1 egg, lightly beaten

1 tsp grated orange rind

1½ tsp dried dill

3 tbsp sunflower oil

* 2 onions, finely chopped

2 carrots, sliced

115 g/4 oz mushrooms, thinly sliced

1½ tbsp paprika, plus extra to garnish

350 ml/12 fl oz beef stock

125 ml/4 fl oz red wine

1 tsp caraway seeds

4 potatoes, cut into chunks

2 tsp cornflour

1 tbsp water

300 ml/10 fl oz soured cream

* salt and pepper

chopped fresh parsley, to garnish

Special

83

Chinese Soup with Meatballs

1. Put the mushrooms into a bowl and pour in warm water to cover. Leave to soak for 15 minutes, then drain and squeeze dry. Discard the stalks and thinly slice the caps.

2. Mix together the beef, onion, garlic, cornflour and egg in a bowl until thoroughly combined. Shape the mixture into small balls, drop them into a bowl of iced water and leave to stand for 15 minutes.

3. Pour the stock into a large saucepan and bring to the boil. Drain the meatballs well, add to the pan and bring back to the boil. Reduce the heat and simmer for 10 minutes. Add the mushrooms, watercress, spring onions and soy sauce to taste and simmer for a further 2 minutes. Serve immediately.

Serves 4–6

5 dried Chinese mushrooms

* 350 g/12 oz fresh beef mince

* 1 onion, finely chopped

* 1 garlic clove, finely chopped

1 tbsp cornflour

1 egg, lightly beaten

850 ml/1½ pints beef stock

1 bunch of watercress (about 25 g/1 oz), stalks removed

3 spring onions, finely chopped

1–1½ tbsp soy sauce

84

Beef Soup with Ginger & Lemon Grass

1. Put the noodles into a bowl and pour in hot water to cover. Leave to soak for 15–20 minutes, until soft. Alternatively, cook according to the packet instructions. Drain the noodles and cut them into 5-cm/2-inch lengths.

2. Put the beef, shallots and 1 tablespoon of the fish sauce into a large bowl, season to taste with pepper and mix well. Cover with clingfilm and chill in the refrigerator until required.

3. Heat half the oil in a large saucepan. Add the rice and ginger and cook over a low heat, stirring constantly, for 1 minute. Pour in the water, increase the heat to medium and bring to the boil. Partially cover the pan, reduce the heat and simmer for 20 minutes, until the rice is tender. Stir in the sugar and the remaining fish sauce and season to taste with salt.

4. Heat the remaining oil in a small frying pan. Add the garlic and lemon grass and cook over a low–medium heat, stirring constantly, for 1 minute, then stir into the saucepan with the noodles and the beef mixture. Bring back to the boil, stirring constantly and breaking up the meat with a wooden spoon. Pour into warmed soup bowls and sprinkle with the peanuts, spring onions and coriander. Serve immediately.

Serves 6

15 g/½ oz dried cellophane noodles

225 g/8 oz fresh beef mince (preferably freshly ground sirloin steak)

2 shallots, finely chopped

4 tbsp Thai fish sauce

2 tbsp groundnut oil

85 g/3 oz long-grain rice

1 tsp grated fresh ginger

1.5 litres/2¾ pints water

1 tbsp brown sugar

2 garlic cloves, very finely chopped

1 tbsp very finely chopped lemon grass

2 tbsp crushed unsalted roasted peanuts

2 spring onions, thinly sliced

1 tbsp chopped fresh coriander

salt and pepper

Beef & Pine Kernel Triangles

1. Heat the oil in a large frying pan. Add the onion and garlic and cook over a low heat, stirring occasionally, for 5 minutes, until softened. Stir in the ground coriander and cumin and cook, stirring occasionally, for a further 3 minutes. Add the beef, half the mint and the pine kernels, increase the heat to medium and cook, stirring and breaking up the meat with a wooden spoon, for 8–10 minutes, until evenly browned. Season to taste with salt and remove the pan from the heat.

2. Meanwhile, cook the potatoes in a saucepan of salted boiling water for 15–20 minutes, until tender but not falling apart. Drain the potatoes, tip into a bowl and mash well, then stir in the cheese until melted. Stir in the beef mixture.

3. Preheat the oven to 200°C/400°F/Gas Mark 6. Brush two baking sheets with a little of the melted butter. Brush one sheet of filo with a little melted butter, put a second sheet on top and brush with more melted butter. Cut the double layer lengthways into three strips. Put a heaped tablespoon of the filling near one end of a strip, then fold over the corner to form a triangle. Continue to fold over in triangles to make a neat parcel, then place on a prepared baking sheet. Make 14 more triangles in the same way. Brush the triangles with the remaining melted butter and bake in the preheated oven for 8–10 minutes, until golden brown.

4. Meanwhile, stir the remaining mint into the tomato sauce and reheat gently. Serve the pastry triangles with the tomato sauce.

Makes 15

1 tbsp olive oil

* 1 small onion, chopped

* 2 garlic cloves, finely chopped

1 tsp ground coriander

1 tsp ground cumin

* 300 g/10½ oz fresh beef mince

4 tbsp chopped fresh mint

2 tbsp pine kernels

2 potatoes, cut into chunks

55 g/2 oz Kefalotiri or Cheddar cheese, grated

115 g/4 oz butter, melted

10 sheets filo pastry

1 quantity Tomato Sauce (see page 58)

* salt

Beef & Onion Piroshki

1. For the dough, sift the flour and salt into a bowl. Add the cream cheese and butter, then rub in with your fingertips until the mixture resembles breadcrumbs. Add 1 tablespoon of the water and mix in, then add 1 tablespoon of the cream and mix in. Repeat twice more. Knead gently, adding a little more water if necessary, then shape into a ball, cover and chill in the refrigerator for 30 minutes.

2. Meanwhile, melt the butter in a saucepan. Add the onion and cook over a low heat, stirring occasionally, for 5 minutes, until softened. Add the beef, increase the heat to medium and cook, stirring frequently and breaking it up with a wooden spoon, for 8–10 minutes, until evenly browned. Remove the pan from the heat, stir in the rice, soured cream, Worcestershire sauce, caraway seeds and chopped egg and season to taste with salt and pepper.

3. Preheat the oven to 200°C/400°F/Gas Mark 6. Grease two baking sheets with butter. Roll out the dough to a thickness of about 3 mm/⅛ inch on a lightly floured surface. Stamp out rounds with an 8-cm/3¼-inch plain cutter. Put a teaspoon of the filling on each round. Brush the edges of the rounds with beaten egg, then fold the dough over the filling and press the edges to seal. Crimp the edges with a fork. Place on the prepared baking sheets and brush with the remaining beaten egg. Bake in the preheated oven for 20 minutes, until golden brown. Serve immediately.

Makes 40–45

55 g/2 oz butter, plus extra
   for greasing

1 onion, finely chopped

225 g/8 oz fresh beef mince

55 g/2 oz cooked rice

2 tbsp soured cream

1 tsp Worcestershire sauce

1 tsp caraway seeds

1 hard-boiled egg, chopped

1 egg, beaten with 1 tsp water

salt and pepper

Dough

350 g/12 oz plain flour,
   plus extra for dusting

pinch of salt

55 g/2 oz cream cheese

115 g/4 oz butter

about 3 tbsp water

3 tbsp double cream

87

Beef & Wild Rice

1. Preheat the oven to 180°C/350°F/Gas Mark 4. Drain the rice and put it into a bowl. Add the beef, onions, garlic, carrots, mustard and eggs. Season to taste with salt and pepper, then mix well with your hands until thoroughly combined.

2. Spoon the mixture into a 1-kg/2 lb 4-oz loaf tin and smooth the surface. Bake in the preheated oven for 1½ hours, until the juices run clear when a skewer is inserted into the centre.

3. Remove the tin from the oven and pour off any fat. Run a round-bladed knife around the edge of the tin and turn out onto a warmed serving plate. Garnish with sage leaves and serve immediately with the tomato sauce.

Serves 6

115 g/4 oz wild rice, rinsed and soaked overnight in cold water to cover

* 500 g/1 lb 2 oz fresh beef mince

* 2 onions, finely chopped

* 2 garlic cloves, finely chopped

4 carrots, grated

1 tbsp Dijon mustard

2 eggs, lightly beaten

* salt and pepper

fresh sage leaves, to garnish

1 quantity Tomato Sauce (see page 58), to serve

Beef Pilau

1. Heat 3 tablespoons of the oil in a saucepan. Add two thirds of the onions and two thirds of the garlic and cook over a low heat, stirring occasionally, for 5 minutes, until softened. Add the rice, ground cumin, turmeric and coriander and cook, stirring constantly, for 1 minute. Pour in the stock and bring to the boil. Stir well, reduce the heat, cover and simmer for 15–20 minutes, until the rice is tender and the liquid has been absorbed.

2. Meanwhile, put the remaining onion, remaining garlic, the beef, mace, cumin seeds and mint into a bowl. Season to taste with salt and pepper and mix well with your hands until thoroughly combined. Shape into walnut-sized balls.

3. Heat the remaining oil in a frying pan. Add the meatballs and cook over a medium heat, turning occasionally, for 6–8 minutes, until evenly browned and cooked through. Remove from the pan and drain on kitchen paper.

4. Remove the rice mixture from the heat and stir in the butter, then gently stir in the meatballs. Transfer to a warmed serving dish, garnish with coriander sprigs and serve immediately.

Serves 4–6

125 ml/4 fl oz olive oil

3 onions, finely chopped

3 garlic cloves, finely chopped

800 g/1 lb 12 oz long-grain rice

1 tsp ground cumin

1 tsp ground turmeric

1 tsp ground coriander

1.7 litres/3 pints beef stock

600 g/1 lb 5 oz fresh beef mince

pinch of ground mace

1 tsp cumin seeds

2 tbsp chopped fresh mint

115 g/4 oz butter

salt and pepper

fresh coriander sprigs, to garnish

Beef en Croûte

1. Preheat the oven to 180°C/350°F/Gas Mark 4. Grease a 650-g/1 lb 7-oz loaf tin with butter. Put the beef, onions, garlic, breadcrumbs, apples, mustard and parsley into a bowl and mix well. Beat one of the eggs with the stock and add to the bowl. Season to taste with salt and pepper and mix until combined.

2. Spoon the mixture into the prepared tin. Stand the tin in a roasting tin and pour in water to come about halfway up the sides. Bake in the preheated oven for 45 minutes. Remove from the oven and remove the loaf tin from the roasting tin. Cover with greaseproof paper, weigh down lightly with a couple of small food cans and leave to cool completely. Remove the cans and paper and turn out when cold.

3. Preheat the oven to 220°C/425°F/Gas Mark 7. Roll out the pastry on a lightly floured surface to a thickness of 3–5 mm/⅛–¼ inch. Put the meatloaf in the centre, brush the edges of the pastry with water and fold over to enclose the meat completely, trimming off any excess pastry. Put the parcel, seam-side down, on a baking sheet. Roll out the trimmings and use to make decorations. Brush with water and arrange on top of the parcel. Lightly beat the remaining egg and brush it over the parcel, then make 2–3 slits in the pastry.

4. Bake in the preheated oven for 35 minutes, until puffed up and golden brown. Reduce the oven temperature to 180°C/350°F/Gas Mark 4 and bake for a further 10 minutes. Serve immediately.

Serves 4

butter, for greasing

✳ 350 g/12 oz fresh beef mince

✳ 2 onions, finely chopped

✳ 1 garlic clove, finely chopped

55 g/2 oz fresh breadcrumbs

2 tart eating apples, peeled, cored and finely chopped

1 tbsp Dijon mustard

2 tbsp chopped fresh parsley

2 eggs

4 tbsp beef stock

300 g/10½ oz ready-made puff pastry, thawed if frozen

plain flour, for dusting

✳ salt and pepper

90

Italian Croquettes

1. Cook the rice in a large saucepan of salted boiling water for 15–20 minutes, until tender. Drain, rinse with boiling water and return to the pan. Stir in half the butter, the Parmesan and parsley. Spread out on a baking sheet and leave to cool.

2. Meanwhile, melt the remaining butter with the olive oil in a saucepan. Add the shallot and garlic and cook over a low heat, stirring occasionally, for 5 minutes, until softened. Add the beef, increase the heat to medium and cook, stirring frequently and breaking it up with a wooden spoon, for 5–8 minutes, until evenly browned. Stir in the wine and cook for 5 minutes. Reduce the heat and stir in the tomato purée, then cover and simmer for 15 minutes. Season to taste with salt and pepper and remove from the heat.

3. When the rice mixture is cold, shape it into balls about the size of a large egg and make a small hollow in each. Put a spoonful of meat mixture and a cube of cheese in each hollow, then re-shape to enclose the filling completely.

4. Lightly beat the eggs in a shallow dish and spread out the flour in a separate shallow dish. Dip the croquettes first in the egg and then in the flour to coat. Heat enough sunflower oil for deep-frying in a deep-fat fryer to 180–190°C/ 350–375°F, or until a cube of bread browns in 30 seconds. Add the croquettes, in batches, and fry until golden brown all over. Drain on kitchen paper and serve immediately.

Serves 4

300 g/10½ oz long-grain rice
55 g/2 oz butter
2 tbsp grated Parmesan cheese
1 tbsp chopped fresh parsley
1 tbsp olive oil
1 shallot, finely chopped
1 garlic clove, finely chopped
115 g/4 oz fresh beef mince
100 ml/3½ fl oz dry white wine
2 tbsp tomato purée
115 g/4 oz mozzarella cheese, cut into cubes
2 eggs
55 g/2 oz plain flour
sunflower oil, for deep-frying
salt and pepper

French Beef Patties in Red Wine

1. Melt 25 g/1 oz of the butter in a frying pan. Add the onions and garlic and cook over a low heat, stirring occasionally, for 5 minutes, until softened. Transfer the mixture to a bowl, add the beef, oregano, parsley and egg and season to taste with salt and pepper. Mix well with your hands until thoroughly combined.

2. Shape the mixture into four patties, each about 2 cm/¾ inch thick. Dust with the flour, gently shaking off the excess.

3. Melt half the remaining butter with the oil in a frying pan. Add the patties and cook for 3–4 minutes on each side, until cooked to your liking. Using a fish slice, transfer the patties to a serving dish and keep warm.

4. Pour off the fat from the frying pan, then add the wine and bring to the boil over a medium–high heat. Boil until reduced by about half. Meanwhile, dice the remaining butter. Remove the pan from the heat and whisk in the butter, one piece at a time, making sure each piece has been incorporated before adding the next. Pour the sauce over the patties, garnish with parsley and serve immediately.

Serves 4

85 g/3 oz butter
* 2 red onions, finely chopped
* 1 garlic clove, finely chopped
* 650 g/1 lb 7 oz fresh beef mince
½ tsp dried oregano
1 tbsp chopped fresh parsley, plus extra to garnish
1 egg, lightly beaten
55 g/2 oz plain flour
1 tbsp olive oil
150 ml/5 fl oz red wine
* salt and pepper

Beef & Pumpkin Baked with Rice

1. Put the onion, beef, mint and cinnamon into a bowl, season to taste with salt and pepper and mix well until thoroughly combined. Divide the mixture into eight equal portions and shape into small patties.

2. Melt 55 g/2 oz of the butter in a frying pan. Add the patties, in batches if necessary, and cook for 3–4 minutes on each side, until lightly browned. Remove with a fish slice.

3. Preheat the oven to 190°C/375°F/Gas Mark 5. Grease a large casserole with butter. Cook the rice in a large saucepan of salted boiling water for 15–20 minutes, until tender. Drain well and rinse with boiling water.

4. Spoon half the rice into the prepared casserole. Melt the remaining butter and pour half of it over the rice. Put the beef patties on top and cover with the remaining rice. Spread the pumpkin cubes over the top, sprinkle with the sugar and pour over the remaining melted butter. Cover and bake in the preheated oven for 25–30 minutes, until the pumpkin is tender. Serve immediately.

Serves 4

* 1 onion, finely chopped
* 500 g/1 lb 2 oz fresh beef mince
* 1 tbsp finely chopped fresh mint
* ½ tsp ground cinnamon
* 175 g/6 oz butter, plus extra for greasing
* 225 g/8 oz long-grain rice
* 500 g/1 lb 2 oz pumpkin or squash, peeled, deseeded and cut into cubes
* 2 tbsp brown sugar
* salt and pepper

93

Lemon Beef in Walnut Sauce

1. Tear the bread into pieces, put it into a large bowl with the milk and leave to soak for 5 minutes. Add the beef, garlic, lemon rind and egg, season to taste with salt and pepper and mix well until thoroughly combined. Using your hands, shape pieces of the mixture into walnut-sized balls.

2. Melt 55 g/2 oz of the butter in a frying pan. Add the meatballs, in batches, and cook over a medium heat, turning frequently, for 5 minutes, until browned all over. Remove with a slotted spoon.

3. Melt the remaining butter in a large saucepan. Add the onions and cook over a low heat, stirring occasionally, for 5 minutes, until softened. Add the walnuts and cook, stirring frequently, for a further 5 minutes. Pour in the water and bring to the boil. Add the pomegranate juice, lemon juice and sugar, then season to taste with salt and pepper. Reduce the heat and simmer, stirring frequently, for 30 minutes.

4. Add the meatballs to the saucepan and simmer very gently for 1½ hours, until almost all the liquid has been absorbed. Transfer to a warmed serving dish, garnish with strips of lemon zest and serve immediately.

Serves 4

1 slice white bread, crusts removed

2 tbsp milk

✳ 500 g/1 lb 2 oz fresh beef mince

✳ 1 garlic clove, finely chopped

1 tbsp finely grated lemon rind

1 egg, lightly beaten

85 g/3 oz butter

✳ 3 onions, finely chopped

140 g/5 oz walnuts, finely chopped

600 ml/1 pint water

5 tbsp pomegranate juice

1 tbsp lemon juice

1½ tbsp sugar

✳ salt and pepper

strips of lemon zest, to garnish

Beef with Red Pepper, Fruit & Nuts

1. Heat the oil in a large frying pan. Add the onions, garlic, celery and red pepper and cook over a low heat, stirring occasionally, for 5 minutes. Add the beef, increase the heat to medium and cook, stirring frequently and breaking it up with a wooden spoon, for 8–10 minutes, until evenly browned.

2. Add the tomatoes, haricot beans, tomato purée, chilli powder, nutmeg, apples, apricots, almonds and French beans. Season to taste with salt and pepper. Reduce the heat, cover and simmer for 30 minutes, then remove the lid and simmer for a further 10 minutes. Serve immediately, garnished with slivered almonds.

Serves 4

3 tbsp sunflower oil

2 onions, finely chopped

2 garlic cloves, finely chopped

2 celery sticks, chopped

1 red pepper, deseeded and chopped

1 kg/2 lb 4 oz fresh beef mince

400 g/14 oz canned chopped tomatoes

400 g/14 oz canned haricot beans, drained and rinsed

6 tbsp tomato purée

1 tsp chilli powder

½ tsp ground nutmeg

2 tart eating apples, cored and chopped

55 g/2 oz ready-to-eat dried apricots, chopped

2 tbsp slivered almonds, plus extra to garnish

115 g/4 oz frozen French beans, thawed

salt and pepper

Stuffed Beef Rolls

1. Preheat the oven to 180°C/350°F/Gas Mark 4. Put the beef mince, shallot, butter, breadcrumbs, lemon rind and olives into a bowl and mix well. Add the egg, then season to taste with salt and pepper and mix until thoroughly combined. Divide the mixture among the beef slices, then roll up and tie with kitchen string.

2. Heat the oil in a flameproof casserole. Add the beef rolls, in batches, and cook over a low–medium heat, turning occasionally, until browned all over. Remove with a slotted spoon and set aside.

3. Add the onions, garlic and carrots to the casserole and cook over a low heat, stirring occasionally, for 5 minutes. Add the stock, tomatoes and bay leaf and bring to the boil. Remove the casserole from the heat and return the beef rolls to it, then cover and cook in the preheated oven for 1½ hours.

4. Remove the casserole from the oven and lift out the beef rolls. Carefully remove and discard the string and put the rolls on a warmed serving plate. Strain the cooking liquid into a jug, pressing down on the vegetables with the back of a spoon. Taste and adjust the seasoning, adding salt and pepper if needed, then pour the sauce over the beef rolls. Sprinkle with the parsley and serve immediately.

Serves 4

* 175 g/6 oz fresh beef mince
* 1 shallot, finely chopped
25 g/1 oz butter
25 g/1 oz fresh breadcrumbs
grated rind of 1 lemon
6 green olives, stoned and chopped
1 egg, lightly beaten
8 slices topside of beef, each about 5 mm/¼ inch thick
2 tbsp olive oil
2 onions, finely chopped
1 garlic clove, finely chopped
2 carrots, finely chopped
300 ml/10 fl oz beef stock
2 tomatoes, peeled, deseeded and sliced
1 bay leaf
3 tbsp finely chopped fresh parsley
* salt and pepper

96

Minced Beef Stroganoff

1. Heat 2 tablespoons of the oil in large frying pan. Add the onion and garlic and cook over a low heat, stirring occasionally, for 5 minutes, until softened. Add the mushrooms and cook, stirring frequently, for a further 5 minutes. Using a slotted spoon, transfer the vegetables to a plate.

2. Add the remaining oil to the pan, then add the beef and cook over a medium heat, stirring frequently and breaking it up with a wooden spoon, for 5–8 minutes, until evenly browned. Drain off as much fat as possible.

3. Reduce the heat to low, return the vegetables to the pan and stir in the brandy. Cook, stirring occasionally, for 4–5 minutes, until the alcohol has evaporated. Stir in the stock, season to taste with salt and pepper and simmer gently, stirring frequently, for 15 minutes.

4. Stir in the soured cream and parsley and cook for a further minute. Garnish with parsley and serve immediately.

Serves 4

3 tbsp sunflower oil

1 onion, chopped

2 garlic cloves, finely chopped

225 g/8 oz mushrooms, sliced

500 g/1 lb 2 oz fresh beef mince

2 tbsp brandy

150 ml/5 fl oz beef stock

150 ml/5 fl oz soured cream

2 tbsp chopped fresh parsley, plus extra to garnish

salt and pepper

Beef Roulade

1. Heat the oil in a saucepan. Add the onion and garlic and cook over a low heat, stirring occasionally, for 5 minutes, until softened. Add the beef mince, increase the heat to medium and cook, stirring frequently and breaking it up with a wooden spoon, for 8–10 minutes, until evenly browned. Remove from the heat and drain off as much fat as possible. Stir in the herbs, season to taste with salt and pepper and leave to cool.

2. Preheat the oven to 190°C/375°F/Gas Mark 5. Put the beef slices, slightly overlapping, on a sheet of clingfilm. Cover with a second sheet of clingfilm and beat with a meat mallet until thin and joined together. Carefully transfer the beaten beef to a board and gently remove the clingfilm. Spread the beef with the cream cheese.

3. Spoon the beef mixture evenly over the top and roll up, then tie with kitchen string. Put the beef roulade in a roasting tin and brush with the barbecue sauce. Cook in the preheated oven for 1–1¼ hours, until tender.

4. Remove the tin from the oven and transfer the roulade to a board. Remove and discard the string, cut the roulade into slices and serve immediately.

Serves 4

1 tbsp olive oil
* 1 small onion, finely chopped
* 1 garlic clove, finely chopped
* 115 g/4 oz fresh beef mince
1 tbsp chopped fresh parsley
1 tbsp snipped fresh chives
8 slices topside of beef, each about 8 mm/⅜ inch thick
225 g/8 oz cream cheese with garlic and herbs
2 tbsp barbecue sauce
* salt and pepper

Aubergine Rolls

1. Heat 2 tablespoons of the oil in a frying pan. Add the onion and garlic and cook over a low heat, stirring occasionally, for 5 minutes, until softened. Add the beef, increase the heat to medium and cook, stirring frequently and breaking it up with a wooden spoon, for 8–10 minutes, until evenly browned. Pour off as much fat as possible.

2. Return the pan to the heat and add the tomatoes. Season to taste with salt and pepper and simmer gently for 15–20 minutes, until thickened. Remove from the heat and leave to cool. Stir the egg, cheese and nutmeg into the Béchamel sauce, then stir the sauce into the beef mixture.

3. Heat half the remaining oil in a frying pan. Add the aubergine slices, in batches, and cook for a few minutes on both sides, until golden brown. Drain on kitchen paper.

4. Preheat the oven to 180°C/350°F/Gas Mark 4. Brush a baking sheet with oil. Stack three sheets of filo, brushing each with some of the remaining oil. Put half the aubergine slices along one long edge, leaving 5 cm/2 inches at each end. Top them with half the beef mixture, spreading it evenly, and roll up the filo. Repeat to make a second roll.

5. Put the rolls onto the prepared baking sheet and brush with the remaining oil. Bake in the preheated oven for 35–40 minutes, until golden brown. Serve immediately.

Serves 4

100 ml/3½ fl oz olive oil, plus extra for brushing

1 onion, grated

1 garlic clove, very finely chopped

225 g/8 oz fresh beef mince

2 tomatoes, peeled, deseeded and chopped

1 egg, lightly beaten

85 g/3 oz Gruyère cheese, grated

pinch of ground nutmeg

125 ml/4 fl oz Béchamel Sauce (see page 70)

3 aubergines, peeled and cut into 5 mm/¼ inch thick slices

6 sheets of filo pastry

salt and pepper

99

Glazed Beef

1. Brush a 1.4-litre/2½-pint pudding basin with oil. Cut out a round of greaseproof paper and a round of foil 10 cm/4 inches larger than the diameter of the basin. Holding them together, make a 2.5-cm/1-inch pleat in the centre.

2. Put the beef, ham, shallots, breadcrumbs, tomato ketchup and herbs into a mixing bowl. Season to taste with salt and pepper. Add the eggs and mix until thoroughly combined. Spoon the mixture into the prepared basin and cover with the cut-out rounds, foil-side uppermost, and tie with string.

3. Put the basin into a large saucepan and carefully pour in boiling water to come about halfway up the sides. Cover and steam for 3 hours, topping up with boiling water as necessary. Remove the basin from the saucepan. Remove and discard the foil and greaseproof paper and pour off any excess fat. Invert the mould onto a serving plate and leave to cool, then chill in the refrigerator for 1 hour.

4. Pour the water into a small bowl, sprinkle the gelatine over the surface and leave to soak for 5 minutes, until spongy. Pour the gelatine mixture into a saucepan and heat gently until the gelatine has dissolved. Add the stock and tomato purée, season to taste with salt and pepper and heat gently, stirring until combined. Remove from the heat and leave to cool. When the mixture is cool, but not set, brush it all over the mould. Chill in the refrigerator until set.

Serves 4–6

sunflower oil, for brushing

* 500 g/1 lb 2 oz fresh beef mince

500 g/1 lb 2 oz ham, very finely chopped

* 2 shallots, finely chopped

55 g/2 oz fresh breadcrumbs

1 tbsp tomato ketchup

2 tsp chopped fresh thyme

1 tbsp chopped fresh parsley

2 eggs, lightly beaten

3 tbsp water

1 sachet (about 11 g/⅓ oz) powdered gelatine

300 ml/10 fl oz beef stock

1 tbsp tomato purée

* salt and pepper

100

Chinese Noodles with Beef & Shredded Vegetables

1. Put the beansprouts and shredded vegetables into small serving dishes and set aside. Cook the noodles in a large pan of salted boiling water according to the packet instructions, then drain and keep warm.

2. Meanwhile, heat a wok over a medium heat, then add the groundnut oil and swirl it around the pan to heat. Add the spring onions, garlic and ginger and stir-fry for 2 minutes. Add the beef and stir-fry, breaking it up with a wooden spoon, for 5 minutes, until evenly browned. Stir in the sesame oil, soy sauce, rice wine and sugar and cook, stirring constantly, for a further 3 minutes.

3. Mix the cornflour to a paste with the water in a small bowl and add to the wok. Simmer, stirring constantly, until the sauce has thickened and become glossy.

4. Divide the noodles among individual bowls and top with the beef mixture and shredded vegetables. Serve immediately.

Serves 4

500 g/1 lb 2 oz dried egg noodles

3 tbsp groundnut oil

3 spring onions, thinly sliced

2 garlic cloves, finely chopped

1-cm/½-inch piece fresh ginger, finely chopped

350 g/12 oz fresh beef mince

1 tbsp sesame oil

5 tbsp soy sauce

2 tbsp Chinese rice wine or dry sherry

1 tbsp sugar

1 tbsp cornflour

4 tbsp water

salt

To serve

115 g/4 oz fresh beansprouts, blanched

115g/4 oz Chinese leaves, blanched and shredded

115 g/4 oz carrots, blanched and shredded

115 g/4 oz cucumber, shredded

115 g/4 oz radishes, shredded